THIS IS WHERE WE CAME IN

by Alan Ayckbourn

║SAMUEL FRENCH║

Copyright © 1995 by Alan Ayckbourn
All Rights Reserved

THIS IS WHERE WE CAME IN is fully protected under the copyright laws of the British Commonwealth, including Canada, the United States of America, and all other countries of the Copyright Union. All rights, including professional and amateur stage productions, recitation, lecturing, public reading, motion picture, radio broadcasting, television, online/digital production, and the rights of translation into foreign languages are strictly reserved.

ISBN 978-0-573-05106-7

concordtheatricals.co.uk
concordtheatricals.com

FOR AMATEUR PRODUCTION ENQUIRIES

United Kingdom and World
excluding North America
licensing@concordtheatricals.co.uk
020-7054-7298

Each title is subject to availability from Concord Theatricals, depending upon country of performance.

CAUTION: Professional and amateur producers are hereby warned that *THIS IS WHERE WE CAME IN* is subject to a licensing fee. The purchase, renting, lending or use of this book does not constitute a licence to perform this title(s), which licence must be obtained from the appropriate agent prior to any performance. Performance of this title(s) without a licence is a violation of copyright law and may subject the producer and/or presenter of such performances to penalties. Both amateurs and professionals considering a production are strongly advised to apply to the appropriate agent before starting rehearsals, advertising, or booking a theatre. A licensing fee must be paid whether the title is presented for charity or gain and whether or not admission is charged.

This work is published by Samuel French, an imprint of Concord Theatricals Ltd.

The Professional Rights in this play are controlled by Casarotto Ramsay & Associates, Waverley House 7-12 Noel Street, London, London W1F 8GQ, United Kingdom.

No one shall make any changes in this title for the purpose of production. No part of this book may be reproduced, stored in a retrieval system, scanned, uploaded, or transmitted in any form, by any means, now known or yet to be invented, including mechanical, electronic, digital, photocopying, recording, videotaping, or otherwise, without the prior written permission of the publisher. No one shall share this title, or part of this title, to any social media or file hosting websites.

The moral right of Alan Ayckbourn to be identified as author of this work has been asserted in accordance with Section 77 of the Copyright, Designs and Patents Act 1988.

USE OF COPYRIGHTED MUSIC

A licence issued by Concord Theatricals to perform this play does not include permission to use the incidental music specified in this publication. In the United Kingdom: Where the place of performance is already licensed by the PERFORMING RIGHT SOCIETY (PRS) a return of the music used must be made to them. If the place of performance is not so licensed then application should be made to PRS for Music (www.prsformusic.com). A separate and additional licence from PHONOGRAPHIC PERFORMANCE LTD (www.ppluk.com) may be needed whenever commercial recordings are used. Outside the United Kingdom: Please contact the appropriate music licensing authority in your territory for the rights to any incidental music.

USE OF COPYRIGHTED THIRD-PARTY MATERIALS

Licensees are solely responsible for obtaining formal written permission from copyright owners to use copyrighted third-party materials (e.g., artworks, logos) in the performance of this play and are strongly cautioned to do so. If no such permission is obtained by the licensee, then the licensee must use only original materials that the licensee owns and controls. Licensees are solely responsible and liable for clearances of all third-party copyrighted materials, and shall indemnify the copyright owners of the play(s) and their licensing agent, Concord Theatricals Ltd., against any costs, expenses, losses and liabilities arising from the use of such copyrighted third-party materials by licensees.

IMPORTANT BILLING AND CREDIT REQUIREMENTS

If you have obtained performance rights to this title, please refer to your licensing agreement for important billing and credit requirements.

THIS IS WHERE WE CAME IN

First performed at the Stephen Joseph Theatre in the Round, Scarborough, on 4th and 11th August 1990 with the following cast:

FRED	Danny McGrath
NELL	Kate Rhodes James
BETHANY	Clare Clifford
TALITHA	Cecily Hobbs
ALBERT	Robert McCulley
JENKIN	Timothy Kightley
GREAT AUNT REPETITUS	Antonia Pemberton
UNCLE ERRATICUS	Gordon Reid
UNCLE OBLIVIOUS	Guy Nicholls
KEVIN ON KEYBOARDS	John Pattison

Directed by Alan Ayckbourn and Malcolm Hebden
Lighting by Jackie Staines
Original music by John Pattison

CHARACTERS

FRED

The Players

NELL
BETHANY
TALITHA
JENKIN
ALBERT

The Storytellers

GREAT AUNT REPETITUS
UNCLE ERRATICUS
UNCLE OBLIVIOUS
KEVIN ON KEYBOARDS

ACT I

(Somewhere or other.)

(A sign says "Stories told here today at 10.30 a.m." (Or whenever).)

*(**FRED**, a young man, waits by the sign. His clothes, though not of the period as the other characters', should seem neutral and timeless.)*

FRED. *(To no-one in particular.)* I've been waiting here a very long time indeed. *(He reflects.)* At least, I think I have.

*(**NELL**, a young woman of about the same age, enters. She wears simple plain peasant-type, somewhat "fairy-tale" clothes. She carries a bundle containing her costumes and props as do all the StoryPlayers.)*

NELL. *(Seeing **FRED**.)* Oh, hallo.

FRED. Hallo.

NELL. Why, it's... Isn't it...? Yes. Aren't you...?

FRED. Fred.

NELL. No, you're not. Surely you're...?

FRED. Fred. My name's Fred.

NELL. Well. All right, then. I'm Nell.

FRED. How do you do.

NELL. Fred? *(She stares at him.)* Are you sure that's your name?

FRED. Don't start that again, please.

NELL. Strange. It must have been another story, mustn't it?

FRED. What?

NELL. Another time. Yes. It was a happy time, I know that.

FRED. *(Suspecting she is slightly deranged.)* Oh, yes? Good.

NELL. So anyway what story are you in at the moment, Fred?

FRED. Story? I'm not in a story.

NELL. Oh, but you must be.

FRED. What story?

NELL. Whoever's telling it. The story by the person who made you up.

FRED. Made me up? What are you talking about?

NELL. Invented you. The reason you're here is because someone somewhere is telling a story about you. You knew that, surely?

FRED. Someone's telling a story? About me?

NELL. Yes. We're all a part of somebody's story.

FRED. Really? That's your theory of life, is it?

NELL. It's not my theory. How else did we get here? If you don't mind my saying so, you're not very well informed are you, Fred? You don't seem to know much.

FRED. *(Indignantly.)* I know lots of things—

NELL. It's not your fault, I'm not blaming you. Please don't get angry. You can't help it, can you? No, I blame the person who's put you in their story. They've just invented a very, very ignorant character, that's all. It's very thoughtless of them.

FRED. I'm not ignorant. I know plenty of things, never you mind.

NELL. What, for instance? You don't even look as if you know what you're doing here.

FRED. I know what I'm doing here.

NELL. What?

FRED. I'm doing here—waiting—waiting patiently for these stories to start.

NELL. Stories?

FRED. *(Indicating the sign.)* These stories, there. Those.

NELL. Oh, those stories. I see.

FRED. Are they anything to do with you?

NELL. Oh, yes.

FRED. Well when are they going to start? I've been waiting here for ages.

NELL. How long? Exactly?

FRED. *(Puzzled.)* I don't know. Exactly. Does it matter? Hours and hours? Days and days? I don't know. Years and years. For ever.

NELL. For ever after. Fascinating. I'd love to know which one of them it is that's telling you. And why? It's a very weird story indeed.

FRED. Never mind about my story. More to the point, what about your story, then?

NELL. My story? Well, my story is your story. It must be. Or yours is mine, I'm not quite sure. I'm not certain yet if I'm appearing in your story or you're appearing in my story. But the fact is we're both in the same story now. Obviously. And the story is apparently that I should come on here ahead of the others in order to meet you alone. Presumably. Why?

FRED. No idea.

NELL. Why to meet you? There must have been a reason. We shall see, won't we? This must have an ending or they couldn't have started it. How exciting... Which one of them could possibly have told it like this? It must have been one of them...

FRED. One of who?

NELL. Well, either...

(Before she can answer, though, the other **STORYPLAYERS** *enter. They are, in no particular order,* **BETHANY**, **TALITHA**, **JENKIN** *and* **ALBERT**. *Each is dressed, as* **NELL** *is, in the basic costume of the character each most often plays. It would seem thus that* **TALITHA** *usually plays mothers and countrywomen;* **JENKIN**, *princes and noblemen;* **BETHANY**, *witches and sundry villains;* **ALBERT**, *woodcutters, shepherds and assorted mechanicals. Like* **NELL**, *they each carry their own particular bundle of props and costume bits and pieces.)*

Ah! Here they are...

BETHANY. Here we are.

JENKIN. Here we are.

TALITHA. Here we are.

ALBERT. Are we? Thank heavens.

NELL. Everyone, this is Fred.

JENKIN. *(Coolly.)* Oh, yes?

TALITHA. Oh, how lovely. Another character.

BETHANY. *(Looking **FRED** up and down appreciatively.)* Another character. Delicious.

ALBERT. Not before time.

FRED. Hallo...

NELL. Fred, this is Bethany...

BETHANY. Hallo. He seems familiar, doesn't he?

TALITHA. Yes, he does rather. I'm Talitha, hallo.

FRED. *(A bit overwhelmed.)* Hallo.

TALITHA. But I can't think where we could have met him, Bethany, can you?

BETHANY. No. But he's not someone you'd forget, is he, Talitha?

TALITHA. Not at all.

BETHANY. *(To **NELL**.)* What did you say his name was, Nell?

NELL. Fred.

BETHANY. Fred?

TALITHA. Fred?

BETHANY. No.

TALITHA. No.

ALBERT. I knew a Fred once.

NELL. Did you?

ALBERT. *(Indicating* **FRED.***)* But it wasn't this one.

NELL. No?

ALBERT. No, this particular Fred died when he was fifty-seven. Eaten by a giant.

TALITHA. Sad.

JENKIN. Personally, I have never known anyone called Fred, alive or dead. But you are familiar... *(He walks away and starts to unpack his bundle in a distant corner.)*

ALBERT. *(Offering* **FRED** *his hand.)* I'm Albert. How do you do.

FRED. How do you do.

ALBERT. I'm usually a woodcutter. Sometimes a shepherd. Though I also do little tailors and I have a good line in loyal four-legged friends.

FRED. Really.

ALBERT. I'm flexible. Him over there. That's Jenkin. He does the nobs. Posh folk. Princes and noblemen and emperors and that.

FRED. Oh.

ALBERT. That's why he's like he is. He's done them so often he thinks he's a royal himself.

FRED. Good. Well, are we...? Are you all going to tell us a story then? Now you're here?

(They all look at him blankly.)

Please?

ALBERT. Oh, no.

BETHANY. No.

NELL. No.

TALITHA. No.

JENKIN. Certainly not.

BETHANY. We're not the StoryTellers…

NELL. We're StoryPlayers.

BETHANY. Quite different.

TALITHA. Quite, quite different.

ALBERT. Quite, quite, quite different.

JENKIN. Utterly different.

FRED. Oh. I'm sorry.

NELL. You mustn't blame Fred. He doesn't know much. He's terribly, terribly ignorant, actually. It's not his fault. He just doesn't seem to have been given any brains.

FRED. *(Indignantly.)* I've got plenty of brains. Don't you worry. All right then, who is telling these stories, if you're not?

TALITHA. They are, of course.

BETHANY. Who else?

FRED. Who?

NELL. Either Great Aunt Repetitus…

ALBERT. If you like hearing things twice…

TALITHA. Or Uncle Erraticus…

ALBERT. When he can remember to get it right…

BETHANY. Or Uncle Oblivious...

ALBERT. If he can remember anything at all.

TALITHA. He forgot on the way here.

BETHANY. That's why we're late.

NELL. *(To* **FRED.***)* Don't worry, they'll be along shortly.

TALITHA. They're quite elderly.

BETHANY. Extremely elderly.

JENKIN. They're all half dead. Well, I'm ready. I don't know about the rest of you.

TALITHA. Well, now you're going to have to wait, Jenkin, aren't you?

BETHANY. Because the StoryTellers aren't here, are they?

JENKIN. Typical.

ALBERT. We don't even know what story they're going to tell yet, anyway.

JENKIN. I can guess what I'll be doing. Something royal. Bound to be.

BETHANY. Why don't you make one up yourself, Jenkin?

TALITHA. Yes, off you go, Jenkin.

NELL. Come on, Jenkin...

ALBERT. Go for it, Jenkin.

JENKIN. If you think I'm doing anything just so you lot can snigger... I can wait. Anyway, we haven't even got... Where is he?

BETHANY. *(Alarmed.)* Oh, no...

ALBERT. *(Equally so.)* Oh!

NELL. *(Alarmed.)* Oh, no...

JENKIN. *(Equally so.)* Oh!

FRED. What's the matter?

TALITHA. *(Agitatedly.)* Oh, oh, oh...!

NELL. *(To* **JENKIN**.*)* What have you done with him?

FRED. Done with who?

TALITHA. *(In panic.)* Well, it wasn't me, you can't blame me this time.

BETHANY. *(Likewise.)* Well, it certainly wasn't me.

FRED. What's the problem? Who's gone missing?

NELL. Kevin on Keyboards, of course.

JENKIN. They'll be livid. Remember how angry they were last time we lost him.

ALBERT. What are we going to do? What do we do now? They'll be here in a minute. What'll they say?

NELL. Now, don't panic. Listen everyone. He can't be far away. We just have to look for him that's all. Everyone spread out and look for him.

ALBERT. Spread out!

TALITHA. Spread out!

BETHANY. Spread out!

JENKIN. Spread out!

(They all spread out.)

FRED. *(Still mystified.)* I'm still not quite certain who we're looking for.

NELL. Kevin on Keyboards. Who do you think? Honestly! Don't you know anything?

ALBERT. Kevin on Keyboards! Come on call him, you lot.

BETHANY. Kevin on Keyboards!

NELL. Kevin on Keyboards!

TALITHA. Kevin on Keyboards!

JENKIN. Kevin on Keyboards!

FRED. Kevin on Keyboards! *(To* **NELL.***)* What does he look like?

NELL. Well, obviously he looks exactly like…

BETHANY. Shh!

TALITHA. Listen!

ALBERT. Shhh!

JENKIN. Shh! Everyone.

(A distant squeaking noise can be heard approaching, offstage.)

NELL. That's him. *(Calling.)* Kevin on Keyboards!

ALL. *(Shouting.)* Kevin on Keyboards!

(There is the roar of an engine, the squeal of tyres and **KEVIN ON KEYBOARDS** *arrives. He (or it) is a strange assemblage of wires and machinery mounted on an apparently self-propelled trolley. This carries a keyboard with accompanying hardware which controls—or maybe is even controlled by—a battered life-size mechanical figure. From* **KEVIN** *emanate all the noises and musical sounds that we hear from now on.*

Overall he looks as if he's seen better days. He screeches to a halt at the edge of the stage.)

FRED. *(Recovering from the sight.)* What is it?

NELL. Kevin on Keyboards.

ALBERT. This is Kevin. This is his keyboard.

FRED. Is he a StoryTeller?

BETHANY. Not really, no.

TALITHA. But he does help tell the stories, don't you, Kevin?

*(***KEVIN** *presses a note and a voice from somewhere says "You bet I do, honeychile".)*

NELL. Kevin, this is Fred.

FRED. Hallo, Kevin, how do you do.

*(***KEVIN** *presses a key and plays a chorus of "Hallo"s.)*

BETHANY. That's just his way of saying hallo.

TALITHA. I think he likes you.

FRED. *(To* **KEVIN**.*)* You know, he seems familiar. I've met him before.

NELL. Have you? That's interesting. Where?

FRED. I can't think where.

NELL. Try and think, Fred. It could be important.

ALBERT. *(To* **FRED**.*)* Were you ever a woodcutter? Maybe that's where we've met?

FRED. No. I don't think so.

ALBERT. A miller? A blacksmith? A magic shoemaker?

FRED. No. I'm sure I'd have remembered.

NELL. He doesn't remember anything, Albert. Who is he? Why do we all know him?

TALITHA. Someone should have given him some thoughts, surely?

BETHANY. And memories...

TALITHA. And ideas.

BETHANY. Careless. It wouldn't have taken long, would it?

ALBERT. As the Swineherd once said to me... Ideas cost nothing.

NELL. *(Touching FRED lightly on the cheek.)* You poor thing. We'll find out about you. Don't worry.

FRED. *(Frowning, taking her hand.)* Nell...?

NELL. Yes? What is it, Fred?

FRED. Nell... Oh, Nell... *(He looks round the group.)* Bethany...?

BETHANY. Yes.

FRED. Talitha?

TALITHA. Yes.

BETHANY. He's remembering...

NELL. Sssh!

FRED. Albert...?

ALBERT. That's me.

FRED. Jenkin...?

JENKIN. Yes.

NELL. Who are you? Who are you really, Fred...

FRED. I'm... I'm... I'm... *(He stops.)*

BETHANY. It's no good, he can't remember...

TALITHA. Maybe there's nothing to remember...

ALBERT. Maybe he wanted to forget...

JENKIN. He's probably nobody anyway...

NELL. He must be somebody. Everybody's somebody. If only we...

(KEVIN plays a fanfare.)

ALBERT. Here they come!

BETHANY. Here they come!

TALITHA. Here they come!

JENKIN. Here they come!

NELL. They're coming!

(The STORYPLAYERS all stand back respectfully. FRED follows suit.)

(Almost immediately three incredibly old people arrive. They appear to be supporting each other. They stop in the doorway, exhausted. They are GREAT AUNT REPETITUS who, predictably, tends to repeat herself and tell circular tales. Supporting her (or maybe supported by her) on either side: UNCLE OBLIVIOUS who falls asleep a lot and forgets where he is in his stories and UNCLE ERRATICUS who stays wide-awake but gets it all wrong. They all stare round looking rather startled for a second. During the following they rest, motionless.)

*(The **PLAYERS** also stand motionless, waiting.)*

FRED. *(In a normal voice.)* Are they the one's who'll be telling—?

PLAYERS. *(Sharply.)* Sssshhh!

FRED. *(More quietly, to **NELL**.)* Are these the ones who'll be telling the stories?

NELL. *(Whispering.)* Yes, of course. They're telling this story now.

FRED. *(Whispering.)* Are they?

NELL. *(Whispering.)* Yes.

FRED. *(Whispering.)* I can't hear them.

BETHANY. *(Whispering.)* In their heads. It's in their heads.

TALITHA. *(Whispering.)* All this is going on in their heads.

ALBERT. *(Whispering.)* We mustn't disturb their concentration.

FRED. *(Whispering.)* Mustn't we?

NELL. *(Whispering.)* No.

FRED. *(Whispering.)* Why not?

JENKIN. *(Whispering.)* Because we'd all disappear, you fool.

ALBERT. *(Whispering.)* We're only pigments of their imagination, you see.

FRED. *(Whispering.)* I'm not a pigment.

BETHANY. *(Whispering.)* Figments not pigments.

FRED. *(Whispering.)* I'm not a figment, either.

(The elderly trio suddenly animate again.)

G-AUNT R. Here we are, then.

UNCLE E. Here we are.

UNCLE O. Here we are.

G-AUNT R. Time for stories!

UNCLE E. Stories!

UNCLE O. Stories!

*(A fanfare from **KEVIN ON KEYBOARDS**. The three **STORYTELLERS** hobble to their positions outside the acting area where they seat themselves. The **PLAYERS** gather at the edge of the stage, and wait expectantly. **FRED** stands with them.)*

ALBERT. *(As they do this.)* Here we go then.

FRED. Great!

TALITHA. I hope it's one with a pretty princess...

BETHANY. *(Sourly.)* One that falls asleep for a hundred years if I've anything to do with it...

ALBERT. Oh, now you two, don't squabble.

G-AUNT R. And the first story will be told by... *(She pauses dramatically.)*

NELL. Wait for it!

G-AUNT R. Uncle Erraticus!

*(A groan from the **PLAYERS**.)*

JENKIN. Oh no, really.

BETHANY. Oh!

TALITHA. Oh!

NELL. Oh, dear!

ALBERT. *(Cheerily.)* Never mind. We'll muddle through. We usually do, don't we?

JENKIN. Muddle's the word.

FRED. Is there a problem?

NELL. Uncle Erraticus always gets everything wrong…

FRED How do you—?

(But before he can ask another question, **KEVIN ON KEYBOARDS** *plays another fanfare.)*

UNCLE E. This is the story of Grethel and Hansel…

NELL. See what I mean?

TALITHA. *(Disappointed.)* Oh…

JENKIN. Oh, Lord… There's nobody royal in this at all.

BETHANY. There's a great witch…

ALBERT. Great story! Great story!

(The **PLAYERS** *scramble to gather up their props and bits of costume.* **ALBERT** *puts on a hat and holds a woodcutter's axe.* **TALITHA** *puts on an apron.* **BETHANY** *goes and lurks in one corner of the stage and dons her witch's attire.* **JENKIN** *and* **NELL** *sit on the floor and attempt to look like children.)*

FRED. *(To* **NELL.** *)* What shall I do?

NELL. You'd better sit and watch. They'll call you if they need you, I expect.

UNCLE E. Once upon a time, on the edge of a large forest—

(**KEVIN** *plays a few bird noises.*)

—lived a very poor couple—and their two children, Grethel and Hansel…

(*The* **PLAYERS** *adopt a family group.*)

NELL. (*Softly.*) So far so good.

UNCLE E. The father was a plumber…

ALBERT. A what?

UNCLE E. And every day he'd go off to work…

ALBERT. Excuse me! I say, excuse me…

UNCLE E. (*Irritably.*) What? What is it?

ALBERT. Excuse me, it's just that he's usually a woodcutter…

UNCLE E. Who is?

ALBERT. The father—he's generally a woodcutter…at least that's—

UNCLE E. Well, he's not. He's a plumber.

G-AUNT R. Don't argue, that person…

ALBERT. Right. I'm sorry. I'm ever so sorry. Just a second. Plumber. That's a very good idea.

(**ALBERT** *dives into his bundle and swaps his axe for a plumber's tool bag. He also changes his woodcutter's hat for a plumber's cap.*)

Right. Ever so sorry. Carry on.

UNCLE E. Are you ready, then?

ALBERT. Yes, yes, sorry.

UNCLE E. I've had trouble with you before, haven't I? Now, where was I?

G-AUNT R. ...lived a very poor couple—

UNCLE E. Oh, yes...and their two children, Grethel and Hansel. The father was a plumber...

(**UNCLE OBLIVIOUS** *has fallen asleep and starts snoring.*)

G-AUNT R. (*Sharply.*) Stop!

(*The* **PLAYERS** *freeze as they always do whenever one of the* **STORYTELLERS** *says this.*)

Oblivious!

UNCLE O. (*Wakening.*) Uh-huh!

G-AUNT R. Oblivious, you mustn't keep falling asleep like that...

UNCLE O. I'm very sorry. I'd no idea I had...

G-AUNT R. Erraticus is telling a story...

UNCLE O. Oh, Lord, is he really...?

UNCLE E. May I be allowed to continue?

G-AUNT R. Yes...

UNCLE E. Have I everyone's permission to continue...?

UNCLE O. Yes, get on with it...

UNCLE E. Thank you... On the edge of this forest lived a very poor couple—and their two children, Grethel and Hansel. The father was a plumber...and every day he'd go off to work in the forest to cut down plum trees.

ALBERT. Oh, flipping heck. *(He goes back to his bundle and swaps his plumber's bag for the axe again. He retains his cap.)*

UNCLE E. *(Furious at this further interruption.)* What are you doing now?

ALBERT. Just a minute, I'm doing my best. Just make up your mind that's all.

UNCLE E. Listen, I've had enough of you...

ALBERT. Look, it's not my fault, is it? First I'm a woodcutter, then I'm a plumber, then I'm a fruit surgeon. I mean, it's not my fault if you keep changing your mind...

UNCLE E. *(Shouting him down.)* Not only was the plum tree cutter very poor indeed, but he'd lost his voice as well...

*(***ALBERT*** mouths on silently, then stops as he realizes.)*

And he lived quietly with his wife, who was the children's stepmother—and was secretly very wicked—

*(***TALITHA*** smirks.)*

—but he had two pretty little children to make up for it.

*(***NELL*** and ***JENKIN*** do their best to oblige.)*

But as time went by, they became poorer and poorer and the food grew less and less. And the stepmother said to the husband:

TALITHA. Husband, how can we possibly feed our poor children when we have nothing left for ourselves?

UNCLE E. And the husband said—

(**ALBERT** *opens and shuts his mouth.*)

—nothing at all. And the wicked stepmother said:

TALITHA. I'll tell you what, I've got one hell of an idea. Tomorrow morning take the children out early into the woods and leave them in the thickest part of the forest. They're so stupid they'll never find their way back so we shall be rid of them. More food for us.

UNCLE E. And their father, who was appalled by this, said—

(**ALBERT** *opens his mouth.*)

—nothing very much. But little did the couple know that upstairs their little boy who was called Grethel—

JENKIN. Grethel...?

UNCLE E. —Grethel had his ear to the floorboards and could hear every word that his parents said. He told his sister Hansel, who wept bitterly.

(**NELL** *weeps bitterly.*)

JENKIN. (*In an undertone.*) I thought I was Hansel...

NELL. (*Similarly.*) Don't argue, keep going...

JENKIN. I'm not strolling around with a name like Grethel...

UNCLE E. What's happening there?

NELL. (*Swiftly.*) Nothing.

JENKIN. (*Equally so.*) Nothing.

UNCLE E. And Grethel comforted his sister Hansel...

FRED. Excuse me. I think you've got them the wrong way round...

UNCLE E. *(Sharply.)* What?

G-AUNT R. Stop!

*(The **PLAYERS** freeze.)*

FRED. It's just their names, I think you've...

UNCLE E. *(Very sharply.)* WHAT?

FRED. Sorry. Carry on.

UNCLE E. And Grethel had a bright idea and he went out into the moonlit garden—

*(**JENKIN** picks up a handful of white pebbles.)*

*(**KEVIN** produces the sound of an owl.)*

—and he gathered up from the ground a handful of bright, shiny saucepan lids...

JENKIN. Saucepan lids. I should have guessed... Hang on...

UNCLE E. What are you doing now?

JENKIN. *(Rummaging in his bag.)* Just a second. *(He finds and holds a pile of saucepan lids.)*

UNCLE E. Everyone's being extremely difficult today...

JENKIN. Sorry to keep you. Here we are.

UNCLE E. *(Glaring at **JENKIN**.)* Unfortunately, as Grethel was gathering them, he banged his leg rather hard...

*(**KEVIN** makes a leg banging noise. **JENKIN** yells and drops the lids with a clatter.)*

UNCLE E. And poor Grethel limped for weeks afterwards. Indeed we shall find out later in the story whether his leg ever got better at all...

(**JENKIN** *gathers up the lids and limps back to his place, scowling.*)

FRED. Excuse me...

UNCLE E. (*Sharply.*) What?

G-AUNT R. Stop!

(*The* **PLAYERS** *freeze.*)

FRED. I don't think they were saucepan lids—

UNCLE E. (*Sharper still.*) What?

FRED. They were stones. Hansel—I mean Grethel—he picked up small white stones...

UNCLE E. Who's telling this story...?

FRED. I—

UNCLE E. Me or you?

FRED. You.

UNCLE E. Then shut up!

FRED. Right.

UNCLE O. Who is that chap?

G-AUNT R. No idea. He seems familiar somehow...

NELL. (*To* **FRED** *in a whisper.*) I shouldn't argue. It's dangerous to argue. They can do terrible things...

JENKIN. (*Rubbing his leg.*) They certainly can...

UNCLE E. And morning came...

(**KEVIN** *plays the dawn chorus.*)

And the wicked stepmother gave each of the children some bread.

TALITHA. Much against her better judgement...

UNCLE E. And said goodbye to them for the last time. And the father with heavy heart led the two children deep into the forest. But little did he know that even as they went, every few yards Grethel would cleverly contrive to drop a saucepan lid—

(**JENKIN** *does so with a clatter.*)

JENKIN. This isn't half as good with saucepan lids...

UNCLE E. (*Viciously.*) Even though the brave little chap's leg still hurt him a good deal...

JENKIN. (*With renewed limping.*) Ow!

UNCLE E. When they reached the middle of the forest, Grethel and Hansel gathered up some wood and their father lit them a fire—

(**KEVIN** *makes a fire crackling noise.*)

—and made them sit there whilst he went off further into the wood, pretending to look for plum trees. But secretly, he crept home.

(**ALBERT** *returns to* **TALITHA** *leaving* **JENKIN** *and* **NELL** *sitting on the ground.*)

And soon it got dark—

(**KEVIN**'s *owl noise again.*)

—and the fire died down—

(**KEVIN**'s *fire noise stops abruptly.*)

UNCLE E. —and the two children huddled together waiting for the moon to rise—which it soon did—

(**KEVIN** *makes a moon rising noise.*)

—and when this happened, Grethel took his sister's hand and followed the trail of saucepan lids that were gleaming so brightly in the moonlight—and they made their way home.

(**NELL** *and* **JENKIN** *gather up the lids as they retrace their steps.*)

And their father, who had never thought to see the children again, was overjoyed to see them.

(**ALBERT** *opens and shuts his mouth.*)

Even though he couldn't say it in so many words. Whilst their stepmother was secretly very angry that they'd found their way home.

TALITHA. *(Sourly.)* Oh goody, it's you two.

UNCLE E. A few days later they were again so short of food and the wicked stepmother said to the plumber:

TALITHA. We've hardly any food at all. You must take those kids back into the woods. And this time lose them properly.

(**ALBERT** *opens and shuts his mouth.*)

UNCLE E. And their father, who was an extremely weak character, said nothing though he was very unhappy about all this. And again Grethel was listening at the floorboards upstairs and heard every word their parents said. And he told Hansel who wept bitterly.

(**NELL** *weeps bitterly.*)

But Grethel said to her:

JENKIN. Fear not, little sister. We can pull the old saucepan lid trick again…

UNCLE E. And he went to creep out into the garden but this time their stepmother had been too clever and had locked the door so he couldn't get out.

(**JENKIN** *tries the door.* **KEVIN** *makes the sound of a rattling lock.* **TALITHA** *laughs.*)

JENKIN. (*As he tries the door: to himself.*) Oh, help.

UNCLE E. And when the dawn came—

(**KEVIN** *repeats the dawn chorus again.*)

—the stepmother gave the children each a piece of bread—

(**TALITHA** *gives them each a tiny piece of bread.*)

TALITHA. —very much against her better judgement—

UNCLE E. —and their father with heavy heart led the children back deeper still into the forest. And this time Grethel, having no saucepan lids, crumbled his piece of bread and left behind a trail of breadcrumbs so that he and Hansel might later find their way home. And when they reached the very thickest part of the wood, Grethel and Hansel again gathered sticks and their father lit them a fire—

(**KEVIN** *repeats the fire crackling sound.*)

—and again he made them sit there whilst he went further into the forest to search for plum trees.

(**ALBERT** *leaves* **NELL** *and* **JENKIN** *as before.*)

And soon it grew dark—

(**KEVIN** *makes his owl noise.*)

UNCLE E. —and their fire died down—

(**KEVIN** *stops the crackling sound.*)

—and the two children waited for the moon to rise so that they could see the trail of bread crumbs and find their way home. And soon the moon rose…

(**KEVIN***'s moon rising noise.*)

But when the children went to search for the breadcrumbs, they found that the birds had eaten them all. They were well and truly lost. Hansel wept bitterly…

(**NELL** *weeps bitterly.*)

JENKIN. Hallo, she's off again…

UNCLE E. And Grethel—despite the fact that his poor little leg still hurt like mad—

JENKIN. Ow! Sorry.

UNCLE E. —comforted her.

JENKIN. (*Doing so.*) There, there, Hansel old thing.

UNCLE E. And they curled up under a pile of leaves and waited till the dawn came…

(**KEVIN** *brings up the dawn chorus.*)

And when they awoke they started to walk again but they soon realized they were hopelessly lost. And then suddenly they came to a clearing and there stood a little cottage all on its own, looking so cosy and inviting. And the children drew closer and saw that the cottage was made not from bricks or stones but from delicious things to eat. And the hungry children rushed forward…

JENKIN. Come on, little sister—

UNCLE E. —cried Grethel—

JENKIN. You tuck in to the roof. I'll start on the walls.

NELL. Yum-yum...

UNCLE E. And indeed the house was delicious. The roof was made of snakes and the walls were made of fingers—

NELL. *(In mid mouthful.)* Yerrk!

JENKIN. *(Likewise.)* Uugg!

UNCLE E. What's the matter now?

FRED. Excuse me... I say...

UNCLE E. What?

G-AUNT R. Stop!

(The PLAYERS freeze.)

FRED. I'm sorry to interrupt again—but I think the roof was made of cakes—not snakes...

UNCLE E. What? What?

FRED. And the walls were ginger not fingers...

UNCLE E. Oh, it's you again, is it?

FRED. Sorry.

UNCLE E. I won't tell you again.

UNCLE O. Who is that chap? Do we know him?

G-AUNT R. I've no idea at all.

UNCLE E. And as they were both nibbling they heard a gentle voice from within calling:

BETHANY. Nibbling, nibbling like a mouse,

Who's nibbling at my little house?

UNCLE E. And suddenly the door opened and a kindly old woman appeared and startled them—

NELL. Oh!

JENKIN. Ah!

BETHANY. Don't be frightened, children. Come inside. I mean you no harm.

UNCLE E. And she led them inside and gave them a huge meal and later on, when it was dark—

(**KEVIN**'s *owl sound again.*)

—she took them both upstairs to two little white beds. And they slept and slept. And as they slept the kindly old woman crept upstairs to look at them and laughed to herself. For she was really not a kindly old woman at all but a wicked witch. And when children strayed into her part of the wood she lured them into her cottage and then fattened them up to eat. For she liked eating children best of all...

(**BETHANY** *cackles.*)

And she seized Grethel and dragged him downstairs and locked him in a cupboard with bars on the door. And then she woke Hansel...

BETHANY. Come on, you lazy slut, fetch some water and cook something nice for your brother. I'm fattening him up to eat.

UNCLE E. Hansel began to cry bitterly...

(**NELL** *cries bitterly.*)

BETHANY. And you can cut that out for starters.

UNCLE E. So whilst Hansel was fed on bones and leftovers, Grethel was fed all the best food in the house. And every day, whilst little Hansel hurried about, the witch would say:

BETHANY. Grethel, put your finger out for me to feel how fat you are.

(**JENKIN** *produces a chicken bone from his bag.*)

UNCLE E. And Hansel instead of sticking out his finger would stick out a phone Instead—

JENKIN. A what?

UNCLE E. —a phone instead—

JENKIN. Yes, that's what I thought you said. Just a minute.

(**JENKIN** *goes to his bag and finds an old fashioned candlestick phone.*)

FRED. Excuse me—

G-AUNT R. Stop!

(*The* **PLAYERS** *freeze.* **UNCLE ERRATICUS** *looks at* **FRED**.)

FRED. Nothing.

UNCLE E. And Hansel instead of sticking out his finger would stick out a telephone instead —

(**KEVIN** *gives a quick phone ring.*)

JENKIN. (*Offering the phone.*) I think it's for you...

UNCLE E. *(Glaring.)* And even as Grethel was doing this, the poor little fellow banged his other leg on the bars.

JENKIN. Ow!

UNCLE E. And the witch whose eyes were dim, could not see that it wasn't his finger and was amazed that Grethel would not get fat...

FRED. I'm not surprised if she's feeding him telephones...

UNCLE E. And how little Hansel wept...

(**NELL** *weeps.*)

Night and day—

(**KEVIN** *gives a very swift owl followed by a dawn chorus.*)

—day and night—

(**KEVIN** *repeats the same in reverse.*)

—until one day the wicked old witch said to Hansel:

BETHANY. Shut up! All right, child, today is baking day. I can't put up with that din a moment longer. I've already heated the oven. Creep inside and tell me if it's warm enough.

UNCLE E. She intended of course, as soon as Hansel was inside, to shut the oven door and roast her. But Hansel pretended not to understand what the witch meant and said:

NELL. I don't know how to get in. How do I get in?

BETHANY. You stupid goose!

UNCLE E. Said the witch.

BETHANY. It's perfectly simple. You get in like this. See?

UNCLE E. And as soon as the witch was halfway into the oven, Hansel gave her a mighty push—

(**BETHANY** *cries out.*)

—slammed the oven door—

(*Sound from* **KEVIN**.)

—and switched it up to gas mark seven. Then Hansel ran and released her brother, crying:

NELL. Grethel, we are saved, saved. The old witch is dead.

UNCLE E. And Grethel said:

JENKIN. Good!

UNCLE E. And they found that the witch's house was filled with jewels and precious stones that she had stolen during her wicked life. And they loaded themselves up with these. And Grethel saw it was time to go home and said to his sister:

JENKIN. It's time to go home.

UNCLE E. And they picked their way back through the enchanted wood. And because it was no longer enchanted it was much easier to find the path. Until that is they came to a stream which looked too deep to cross.

JENKIN. Ah!

NELL. Oh!

JENKIN. Looks too deep to cross.

UNCLE E. But fortunately there was a chicken swimming past—

(**KEVIN** *makes a splash/chicken noise.*)

FRED. It was a duck—

UNCLE E. What?

G-AUNT R. Stop!

(*The* **PLAYERS** *freeze.*)

FRED. It was a duck not a chicken...

UNCLE E. Now listen. I don't know who you are but I've had enough from you.

FRED. Sorry.

UNCLE O. Who is that chap?

G-AUNT R. I keep telling you, I've no idea. And yet...

UNCLE O. Any more arguments?

NELL. No...

JENKIN. No, no. Looks exactly like a chicken to me.

NELL. Oh, look—

UNCLE E. —cried Hansel—

NELL. Maybe that chicken will give us a ride on its back.

UNCLE E. And the chicken said—

(*There is a chicken noise from* **KEVIN**.)

And the children cried:

NELL.
JENKIN. } (*Together.*) Oh, thank you, thank you, chicken!

UNCLE E. And they clambered, each in turn, on the bird's back and she swam with them to the other side of the stream.

(**NELL** and **JENKIN** *both do this with appropriate noises from* **KEVIN**.)

And once safely across they were able to see their own little cottage and they both scampered home and through the gate. And there to welcome them, who else but—

(**ALBERT** *stands beaming at them, arms extended.* **TALITHA** *stands beside them looking appalled.*)

—their dear father who had wept bitterly from the day he had left them. As for their wicked stepmother, as soon as she saw them both, she choked on the bread she was eating and dropped dead on the spot—

(**TALITHA** *gurgles and falls on the floor.*)

—and good riddance to bad rubbish. So the children went inside with their father and showed him all the jewels and precious stones they had brought back with them. And the old plumber cried:

ALBERT. Kids, we're rich...

UNCLE E. And although money isn't everything, it's a lot better than nothing. And although it didn't make them happy all by itself, it certainly helped. It certainly helped Grethel and Hansel and their father, the plumber, to live happily ever after.

(*A final chord from* **KEVIN**.)

(**FRED** *applauds*.)

G-AUNT R. And now—a story from Uncle Oblivious...

(*Another chord from* **KEVIN**. *They all look towards* **UNCLE OBLIVIOUS** *who seems unaware of them, lost in his own thoughts...*)

Oblivious...

UNCLE O. Mmmm?

G-AUNT R. It's your turn...

UNCLE O. My turn for what?

G-AUNT R. Your turn to tell a story...

UNCLE O. Oh, yes. Right. Here we go.

(**KEVIN** *repeats his chord.*)

Yes...

NELL. (*Softly, to* **FRED.**) This could take some time.

JENKIN. (*Softly.*) This could take all night.

FRED. (*Softly.*) Why?

NELL. (*Softly.*) He sometimes can't remember...

BETHANY. (*Softly.*) He can never remember a thing.

TALITHA. (*Softly.*) He's hopeless...

UNCLE O. Here we go then...

(**KEVIN** *plays his chord.*)

This one's called the...oh, dammit...er—whatjamacallit...thingy...the thing thingy...what's it called now?

UNCLE E. Oh, get on with it, man...

UNCLE O. I'm going to...just a tick. Oh, what are they called? Hopping things...?

UNCLE E. Kangaroos?

UNCLE O. Certainly not. Kangaroos? What a stupid suggestion.

G-AUNT R. Oh, do get on with it, Oblivious...

UNCLE O. I'm trying to. People keep interrupting me... er, Prince. Prince. That's the word.

G-AUNT R. Prince? The Prince Who Hopped?

UNCLE O. No, no...

UNCLE E. The Hopping Prince?

UNCLE O. No, no, no. The something Prince. The something-that-hops Prince.

G-AUNT R. Grasshopper?

UNCLE O. The Grasshopper Prince? No, no, no... What else hops?

UNCLE E. A three-legged dog?

UNCLE O. The Three-Legged Dog Prince? No, no, no...

FRED. Frog?

UNCLE O. What? No, I've just said not dog. Didn't you hear me?

FRED. No, Frog.

UNCLE O. Frog?

FRED. Prince. The Frog Prince.

UNCLE O. The Frog Prince. Exactly. What about it?

FRED. Well, was that the story you wanted to tell?

UNCLE O. Well, of course it was if you'll only let me get on with it. *(To the others.)* Who is he?

UNCLE E. No idea.

G-AUNT R. *(Looking keenly at* **FRED.***)* I've seen you before, haven't I?

FRED. No, I don't think so...

UNCLE O. The Frog Prince. In olden times when wishes actually meant something, unlike today when you can wish for things till the cows come home and you might just as well whistle for all the good it'll do you...there lived a king—

JENKIN. *(Donning a crown and steps forward.)* Hallo, there. This is a better part.

UNCLE O. And this particular king had an especially fine line in daughters.

(**TALITHA** *and* **BETHANY** *don crowns and step forward.*)

JENKIN. Hallo, kids.

TALITHA.
BETHANY. } *(In chorus.)* Hallo, Daddy.

UNCLE O. But it has to be said that it was the youngest of them that was the real cracker—

(**NELL** *steps forward.*)

JENKIN. Wotcha, nipper.

NELL. Hi, Daddy.

UNCLE O. Now, near the king's palace there was a large forest...

(**KEVIN** *produces more birdsong.*)

There always is. And in this forest, under an old lime tree, was a deep well...

(**KEVIN** *makes a water-plopping sound.*)

Now, when it was a very hot day, this youngest princess used to go and sit by this cool well. And when she got cheesed off with doing that she used to play with this golden ball she'd had given to her. Chucking it in the air and generally giving it a few brisk overs of right arm spin.

(**NELL** *produces the golden ball and leaps about with it.*)

Now, on this particular afternoon, she was prancing about as usual—the way girls do when they think no-one's watching them—and, of course, the inevitable happened, she dropped one slightly short of a length and before you could say Ray Illingworth the ball had gone and dropped straight down the— oh— *(He breaks off abruptly.)*

(The action freezes. A pause.)

FRED. *(To* **TALITHA**, *in a whisper.)* What's happening?

TALITHA. *(Whispering.)* He's forgotten the next word. We can't go on till he remembers it.

FRED. How long's he going to be?

BETHANY. No idea. Hours, sometimes. He usually falls asleep.

FRED. He can't fall asleep now. I want my dinner. *(Loudly.)* Down the well.

UNCLE O. Eh?

G-AUNT R. Stop!

FRED. Well.

UNCLE O. Well, what?

FRED. Down the well. The ball. Down the well. Fell.

UNCLE O. Down the well, yes. Who's telling this story. Who is he?

G-AUNT R. We've definitely seen him before, you know…

UNCLE E. Yes, I think we have seen him before…

UNCLE O. If I may continue. And before you could say Ray Illingworth the ball had gone and dropped straight down the well.

(*A splash from* **KEVIN**.)

NELL. Oh, botheration!

UNCLE O. Cried the princess. And she began to weep bitterly.

(**NELL** *weeps bitterly.*)

And after a bit, out of the well pops this frog.

(**ALBERT** *dons frog headgear and emerges.*)

ALBERT. Hallo. What's all this ghastly racket about?

UNCLE O. Asked the frog.

NELL. I've lost my golden ball down the well.

UNCLE O. Wept the princess.

ALBERT. Well, you ought to learn to pitch 'em up, then.

UNCLE O. Cried the frog. Who, it has to be said, could turn his arm over himself, if asked to do so…

ALBERT. Line and length, girl. Line and length. Did your mother teach you nothing? Tell you what. If I dive in and fetch it for you, what'll you give me?

NELL. Oh, anything—practically anything.

UNCLE O. Wept the princess.

NELL. My pearls and diamonds. Even the golden—golden—

UNCLE. —golden...thingy—

NELL. —golden...thingy—on my head.

UNCLE O. And the frog said:

ALBERT. I care not for your pearls or your diamonds. Or for the golden thingy on your head. But if you'll be fond of me, let me be your best friend, sit by you at table, eat out of your plate, drink out of your cup and doss down beside you in your little milk-white bed, if you promise me this, I'll fetch your ball for you.

UNCLE O. And the princess replied:

NELL. Oh, yes. Anything, anything you like, if you'll only rescue my ball.

UNCLE O. But secretly she thought:

NELL. Fat chance, froggy face.

UNCLE O. And the frog, as soon as he had her promise, dived beneath the water and returned with her ball.

NELL. Thanks!

(**NELL** *takes the ball and moves off.*)

ALBERT. Wait, wait! What about me? Take me with you.

NELL. Where?

ALBERT. Home. With you. You promised.

NELL. You're joking. I'm not going home with a frog. What would Daddy say? He'd never forgive me.

UNCLE O. And she tossed her pretty head and off she ran—

(**NELL** *does this.*)

Leaving one very disgruntled frog.

ALBERT. Well, really. Some people...

UNCLE O. Now, that same evening, the princess was sitting having dinner with her father, the king—

(**KEVIN** *plays some Royal Dinner Music.* **NELL** *and* **JENKIN** *sit at a table.*)

—when there was this knock at the door.

(*There is one.*)

JENKIN. Who on earth can that be? It's quarter-past seven.

UNCLE O. Said the king.

TALITHA. (*Now a maid.*) Excuse me, Your Majesty, Sir, Your Royal Highness, Madam, but there's a frog at the door to see you, Madam, Your Royal Highness.

NELL. Oh, no.

JENKIN. Who is it? A frog did you say, Potter?

TALITHA. Yes, Your Royal Majesty.

JENKIN. Well, tell him to go away. The princess is having her pilchards...

NELL. Yes, tell him to go away, Petherbridge.

TALITHA. He's very insistent, Your Royal Highness, Madam. He's hopping up and down something terrible.

JENKIN. Why should he be doing this, daughter? Any idea? Do you owe him money?

NELL. No, no. I made him this silly promise. It was nothing.

JENKIN. What promise?

UNCLE O. And the princess told her father all about the promise she had made to the frog.

JENKIN. Well, in that case we'd better haul him in then.

UNCLE O. Said the king.

NELL. Oh, Daddy, no...

JENKIN. A promise is a promise, isn't it? Eh? Pour him in, Peters...

TALITHA. Yes sir, Your Majesty, Sir.

NELL. Oh, Daddy...

JENKIN. No fair's fair...

NELL. What are we going to have to talk about?

TALITHA. The frog, Madam.

ALBERT. Evening.

JENKIN. Fetch the frog a whatsit, Perkins.

ALBERT. Much obliged.

JENKIN. And put the whatsit—chair—that's the word—next to Her Royal Highness, Povey.

TALITHA. Yes, Your Highness Majesty, Sir.

NELL. Oh, Daddy, no, no, no!

TALITHA. Pardon me, Your Highness Royal, Madam.

ALBERT. Thanks very much. Actually, I think I'll be better off on the table, if it's all the same. Easier to share your plate from here. *(He climbs on the table.)*

NELL. What are you doing? Get your feet out of my pilchards.

ALBERT. Pilchards. Oh, grand.

UNCLE O. Said the frog.

ALBERT. I wonder, would you mind pushing your golden plate a bit closer? So's we can share them.

NELL. Certainly not.

JENKIN. Do as he says, girl. A promise is a promise.

UNCLE O. And so the princess finished up sharing her dinner with the frog. Though it has to be said she didn't eat much of it herself. Whereas the frog really tucked in. Not only polished off her pilchards but drank most of her Tizer.

ALBERT. Well, that was champion. Thanks very much. *(He belches.)* Well, I don't know about you, lass, but I think I could do with a lie down and a spot of kip. Coming up, are you?

NELL. Certainly not!

JENKIN. Do as he tells you, girl.

NELL. Daddy, no, no, no, no, no...

JENKIN. A promise is a promise.

NELL. But I'm not getting into bed with a frog. I couldn't.

JENKIN. Well, you should have thought about that before you made these promises...

NELL. But I'd lost my ball...

JENKIN. Well, you shouldn't have done, should you? If you'd learnt to pitch it up like I taught you—

ALBERT. Wrong line. She was bowling a wrong line, too.

JENKIN. Well, there's something basically wrong with her run up, there always has been. She's running wide of the crease, you see. If she only ran closer to the stumps...

ALBERT. She'd have a better line...

JENKIN. She would. Now her older sister, my middle one, Enid, she's a promising little quickie—

ALBERT. Is she? Is she, now?

JENKIN. Just short of a length, bangs them in. Easy run up, nice action, fast medium...

TALITHA. Great ground fielder, too...

NELL. All right, all right! Let's go to bed, then. If you're going to talk cricket all night...

ALBERT. Thanks very much. Going to give us a carry?

NELL. No, I'm damn well not. You can hop.

JENKIN. Porterhouse, carry the frog upstairs.

BETHANY. Yes Sir, Your Royal Majestic Highness, Sir...

JENKIN. Good-night, daughter...

NELL. *(Kissing him.)* Good-night, Daddy. *(To **ALBERT**.)* Come on. I hope she drops you downstairs.

UNCLE O. And so very reluctantly the princess went upstairs to her pretty little milk-white bed—followed by the maid with the frog. And the princess sat in front of her mirror and brushed her long flowing hair with her hatstand...

NELL. Hatstand? *(She shrugs.)* Put him down over there, Pattison. He can sleep over there. In the corner.

ALBERT. In the corner? What about the bed?

NELL. Certainly not. That is my bed. You're not sleeping in that. Not between my pretty little milk-white sheets, you're not.

ALBERT. I'm not sleeping in the corner. Why don't you sleep in the corner?

NELL. Because. That is my bed, frog!

ALBERT. You promised I could have the bed.

NELL. Well, you can't. Now stay over there or I'll throw my hatstand at you. You may go, Pullborough.

(**TALITHA** *withdraws.*)

UNCLE O. And without another word the princess climbed into bed, whilst the frog sat in the corner watching her. And after a little time, she fell asleep. And the full whatsisname rose in the sky—

(**KEVIN** *makes an owl noise.*)

And the frog crept over and sat on the side of her bed.

ALBERT. Hallo, then.

NELL. *(Waking.)* Wah!

ALBERT. It's all right. It's only me. And I've hidden your hatstand, so don't try it.

NELL. I shall scream, I warn you.

ALBERT. Oh, come on. Give us a kiss.

NELL. Certainly not.

ALBERT. Come on.

NELL. I could catch all sort of—frog things.

ALBERT. You promised.

NELL. Didn't.

ALBERT. Did. I'll tell your dad.

(Pause.)

A promise is a promise, remember.

NELL. You bully! You great—bullying—bullfrog…!

UNCLE O. And very, very, very reluctantly indeed she leant forward and—kissed the frog…

NELL. *(As she does so.)* Yeurrk!

UNCLE O. But even as they touched—

*(Dramatic chord from **KEVIN**.)*

—there was a puff of wool, a great rushing of thing and a flash of thunder which hurled them both apart—and lo and behold when the princess opened her eyes the frog had been transformed into a—a handsome…oh, dammit what's the word—oh—what's the matter with me these days? —er…an incredibly handsome…

FRED. *(Standing up.)* Prince.

UNCLE O. Prince. Exactly. Well done, that man. And the princess, as soon as she saw the young prince, fell immediately in love with him…

NELL. *(Falling immediately in love.)* Oh!

FRED. Thank you. I am Prince Florizel and you have saved me from a witch's curse. Only you could do this.

NELL. Oh.

UNCLE O. *(A bit startled.)* Just a minute, who are you?

FRED. I am yours forever.

NELL. And I am yours...

(NELL and FRED stand gazing into each other's eyes adoringly.)

UNCLE O. And they both lived happ—Who is that chap? He wasn't supposed to be in this story...

G-AUNT R. Stop! Oh, now I know who that is...

UNCLE E. So do I, now...

G-AUNT R. It's him...

UNCLE E. It's him...

UNCLE O. Good Lord. Him...

TALITHA. Who is he?

G-AUNT R. *(Sharply.)* Mind your own business.

UNCLE O. What are we going to do?

G-AUNT R. It's a bit late to ask that now, isn't it?

UNCLE O. But he can't stay, can he? He's dangerous.

UNCLE E. It's your fault, Oblivious, for putting him in your stupid story...

UNCLE O. It wasn't my fault. I forgot.

UNCLE E. Forgot? He'll be in all the stories now, don't you see? We'll never get him out again, you idiot...

UNCLE O. Don't call me an idiot, how was I to know...

UNCLE E. Idiot! Idiot! You'll forget your head...

G-AUNT R. Stop that at once! Stop it! STOP IT!

(Silence.)

That's better. What behaviour. Men of your age.

UNCLE O. But what are we going to do, Great Aunt?

G-AUNT R. It's very simple, Oblivious. We don't panic. That's the first thing. All we need do—is—

(She looks up and is aware that the **STORYPLAYERS** *are all listening.)*

Just a moment. *(Narrating.)* And all around the palace both inside and out a strange sleep descended on everyone, man, woman and child...

(All the **STORYPLAYERS** *fall asleep where they stand.)*

That's better. Now they can't hear us. It's very simple. All we need do—all I need to do—is to tell a story with the boy in it—in which he'll—disappear...

UNCLE O. Disappear?

G-AUNT R. For ever.

UNCLE E. Can you make that happen?

G-AUNT R. Of course I can. I promise you—by the time I've finished my story—he'll never be seen again. Ever.

UNCLE O. I hope it works. If he starts his...

G-AUNT R. It'll work...

UNCLE O. If he starts his...

G-AUNT R. *(Sharp.)* I said it'll work. That's enough. Leave it to me. *(Narrating.)* And the following morning—

*(***KEVIN** *plays some birdsong.)*

G-AUNT R. —thank you, Kevin—they all awoke from a deep refreshing sleep...remembering nothing of what they had heard before they slept...

(*The* **STORYPLAYERS** *all awake.*)

NELL. Fred...

FRED. Hallo, I...

NELL. What are you doing there?

JENKIN. Yes, what exactly are you doing there? Get off at once.

TALITHA. Off...

BETHANY. Get off!

NELL. You're not supposed to be here, Fred, if you're not in the story...

FRED. Sorry.

G-AUNT R. Oh, but he is, child. He is in the story, you see.

NELL. Fred? Fred is in the story?

G-AUNT R. That's not his name, either. He's a Story Player like you and his real name is Flavius.

NELL. Flavius? Flavius!

(*The other* **PLAYERS** *look at her sharply.*)

G-AUNT R. Come here, child. What do you know about Flavius?

NELL. Nothing, Great Aunt.

UNCLE E. Have you ever heard that name before?

NELL. No.

UNCLE O. You don't remember it from anywhere?

NELL. No. I've—never heard it...

G-AUNT R. Are you sure?

NELL. Yes, Great Aunt.

G-AUNT R. Have any of you ever heard the name Flavius before?

(All the **STORYPLAYERS** *hastily deny it.)*

(Looking at them suspiciously.) No. I hope not. We'll pause there for a little while before the next story which will be mine. And since Flavius is our newest recruit, it's a story that will concern him a good deal. I look forward to that. Come. *(She rises and reaches out her hands.)*

*(***ERRATICUS** *and* **OBLIVIOUS** *move to her. Together they move out during the following.)*

In the meantime, all of you, I should rest. It's going to be a very busy story for you all. Plenty of excitement, I can promise you that. *(She laughs to herself.)*

(The three go off, laughing.)

(The others look at **FRED.***)*

NELL. I can't believe it. You're really—?

BETHANY. Shhh!

TALITHA. Don't even say the name.

BETHANY. Don't speak it.

JENKIN. We're not supposed to remember it.

ALBERT. It's all right to say it now. They've just told us it, haven't they? They thought we'd forgotten.

FRED. What is this about? I—

NELL. He still doesn't remember.

BETHANY. There is a secret legend, amongst all StoryPlayers, that at one time the Players told their own stories, freely, as they wanted to tell them.

TALITHA. But a few of them, a powerful few, banded together and in time became the StoryTellers…

ALBERT. Like those three. And from then on, only they, the Tellers, could tell the stories.

JENKIN. They controlled the Players who lost all their power…

FRED. I see. Then who's—?

NELL. There was apparently one player… who defied them. He continued to tell his own stories…

BETHANY. His name was Flavius.

JENKIN. That's your name.

FRED. Me? But I'm not a Player, I'm—

TALITHA. He still can't remember a thing…

ALBERT. The StoryTellers got very angry, you see. So they put this feller into a story…

JENKIN. A story where he was made to vanish…

FRED. Vanish? Where?

JENKIN. Nobody knows. To ever after somewhere, I suppose. Nobody even remembers the story or who told it.

BETHANY. The point is, none of us were ever meant to remember him. The story ended with us forgetting him. But we never did.

ALBERT. Really.

TALITHA. Any of us.

JENKIN. Quite.

NELL. Ever. Ever.

(A pause.)

FRED. *(Looking at them.)* Well, if I am this—this Flavius bloke...what am I supposed to do...

NELL. Heaven knows how, but you've been given another chance to save us, Flavius.

TALITHA. Rescue us...

JENKIN. Lead us out of their stories...

BETHANY. So we can tell our own...

NELL. Help us...

TALITHA. Please...

BETHANY. Please...

FRED. *(Nervously.)* Well. How should I go about it, do you think?

ALBERT. They're planning to put you in a story. It'll be a test of strength. If you are Flavius—then you might just be strong enough to fight them...

FRED. *(Flustered.)* Yes, OK. If you think so. I could have a go, I suppose.

BETHANY. Wonderful.

TALITHA. Marvellous.

ALBERT. Great.

JENKIN. Goodman.

NELL. Thank you, Flavius.

FRED. No harm in that, is there? Can't be dangerous? Can it?

JENKIN. Oh, yes, it can be very dangerous, Flavius.

NELL. They'll try and make you disappear, Flavius.

FRED. Where...whereabouts...

ALBERT. Oh. Ever after. Who knows?

FRED. Like in happily ever after, you mean?

ALBERT. Not necessarily. See you later, Flavius. Beware, that's all. *(He moves to leave.)*

JENKIN. Beware! *(He follows **ALBERT**.)*

BETHANY. Beware! *(She follows **JENKIN**.)*

TALITHA. Beware! *(She follows **BETHANY**.)*

NELL. *(Kissing him lightly.)* Beware, Flavius! *(She follows **TALITHA**.)*

*(The **PLAYERS** leave.)*

*(**FRED** stands a little nervously.)*

FRED. Well — I'll come back next week, I suppose. I suppose so. *(To **KEVIN**.)* What do you think I should do?

*(**KEVIN** touches his keyboard. A deep hollow voice booms "Beware!" followed by a sinister hollow laugh.)*

*(**FRED** rushes off.)*

*(**KEVIN** also trundles away, still laughing.)*

(Curtain.)

ACT II

(The same somewhere or other.)

*(**FRED** waits by the sign that says, "Stories told here today at 10.30 a.m." (or whenever) as before.)*

FRED. *(To no one in particular.)* I've been waiting here a very long time indeed. *(He reflects.)* At least, I think I have.

*(**NELL** enters rather furtively.)*

NELL. Flavius...

FRED. Oh, there you are. I wondered where you'd all got to.

NELL. Sorry. I think the Story Tellers managed to split us all up somehow.

FRED. How? How did they do that?

NELL. That's the way they told it. Whatever they tell happens. You find yourself doing things whether you like them or not.

FRED. Maybe you do. I don't. I make up my own mind.

NELL. Be careful. That's what they'd like you to believe. You may only think you are—

FRED. Really?

NELL. You need to be on your guard, all the time.

FRED. Me?

NELL. Especially you. Being who you are.

FRED. What have they got against this bloke, whatsisname, Flavius...?

NELL. Shh! Because while you're alive—you're a danger to them, don't you see? You're the only StoryPlayer who ever, *ever* managed to stand up to the StoryTellers. Who nearly succeeded in taking their power away from them and returning it to the Players where it belongs. You so nearly managed it...

FRED. Did I? But I didn't, did I? And what makes you all think I'm him, anyway? He's dead, isn't he? And I'm alive. His name is Flavius; my name is Fred.

NELL. Flavius was—you were never dead, you were...

FRED What?

NELL. You were—ever after—

FRED. Ever after?

NELL. That's the only way to say it. Out of the stories. Where all the characters go when they've finished with them.

FRED. Ever after?

NELL. Right.

FRED. Happily ever after?

NELL. Some of them, yes.

FRED. *Unhappily* ever after?

NELL. Some of them, yes.

FRED. I can guess where I was.

NELL. You still can't remember?

FRED. Not a thing. Anyway, what am I doing back here? Why aren't I still living unhappily ever after?

NELL. I don't know. It could be a number of things.

FRED. Like? Like? You have to tell me. If they're going to try and send me back, I need to know what I'm doing here. What brought me back again?

NELL. Well—it could have been Uncle Erraticus. He does get things wrong quite a lot. He may have brought you back by mistake. Or—possibly it was Uncle Oblivious... He could have forgotten you ever existed and somehow reinvented you...

FRED. Or Great Aunt Whatsername? Could she have had anything to do with it?

NELL. Great Aunt Repetitus? It's unlikely. She never usually makes mistakes. She's too clever. Far and away the most dangerous. Whatever you do, be careful of her. She'll be telling the story today.

FRED. I'll be careful of all of them. Hey—

NELL. What?

FRED. If they write everything...?

NELL. Practically everything...

FRED. How do we know they haven't written this bit?

NELL. We don't know for sure.

FRED. So the chances are the conversation we've just been having they might have invented anyway. In which case there'd be no point in having the conversation. In which case—oh, this is all too complicated for me...

NELL. I've told you—they don't invent everything...

FRED Well, how do we know what they don't—

(**NELL** *kisses him.*)

(*Startled.*) Wha—?

NELL. (*Smiling.*) Nobody else invented that, I promise you. (*She stops and listens.*) Someone's coming. Oh, it's the others...

(**BETHANY, TALITHA, ALBERT** *and* **JENKIN** *come on. They carry their bundles of props and costumes, as previously.*)

Ah! Here they are...

BETHANY. Here we are.

JENKIN. Here we are.

TALITHA. Here we are.

ALBERT. Are we? Thank heavens.

BETHANY. (*Looking at* **FRED.**) Is he ready?

NELL. He's ready.

FRED. I'm ready.

TALITHA. Good luck—Flavius.

FRED. I'm ready for anything.

JENKIN. Frightened of nothing, eh?

FRED. Frightened of nothing—

ALBERT. —and no-one—

FRED. —and no-one—

NELL. Here's to Flavius!

ALL. *(Except* **FRED**, *in a whisper.)* Flavius!

*(***FRED** *stands impressively. We hear the roar of a car engine and the scream of brakes.* **FRED** *jumps a mile.)*

*(***KEVIN ON KEYBOARDS** *comes on as before, keyboard screaming to a halt.)*

BETHANY. Good-afternoon, Kevin on Keyboards.

*(***KEVIN** *presses a note. A hollow voice booms "Beware!" as before, followed by sinister laughter.)*

FRED. Yes. Very funny.

ALBERT. The others must be on their way. Listen, Flavius—er—I don't know how to put this but—once the story starts—once things get underway—you may be on your own, mate. You understand?

FRED. How do you mean?

JENKIN. He means that once we get into the story, most of us most of the time won't be responsible for our own actions. Do you see?

BETHANY. We'll do what we can to help...

TALITHA. Everything we can...

JENKIN. But trust none of us. *(Indicating* **BETHANY.***)* Especially her.

ALBERT. Especially her.

BETHANY. Especially me.

ALBERT. *(Talking to* **FRED** *like a boxing second.)* You're on your own. Keep moving, that's the secret. Don't let them settle. They'll try and set up a pattern, you see...

FRED. A pattern, yes...

JENKIN. You've got to break the pattern. Break it, you see?

FRED. *(Trying to take all this in.)* Break it, yes.

ALBERT. They'll try and lull you into a false sense of security, you see?

FRED. Security, yes.

JENKIN. If you let them do that, you're done for...

ALBERT. So keep your guard up...

JENKIN. Don't let them get you into a corner...

BETHANY. Lookout!

(They scatter to the corners of the stage. **FRED** *stays with* **NELL** *for a second longer.)*

FRED. Nell, can't I even trust you?

NELL. I hope you can, Flavius. I'll try. But I can't guarantee it. None of us can. But just remember the one other reason that could have brought you back. The strongest reason of all of them.

FRED. What's that?

NELL. Love, Flavius. Love.

*(***KEVIN*** plays a fanfare.)*

(The three **STORYTELLERS** *enter, as before.* **GREAT AUNT REPETITUS** *supported on either side (or perhaps supporting)* **UNCLE ERRATICUS** *and* **UNCLE OBLIVIOUS**.*)*

G-AUNT R. Story time, then.

UNCLE E. Story time.

UNCLE O. Story time.

G-AUNT R. And my turn, I think...

*(The **STORYTELLERS** shuffle to their respective places off the acting area. The **STORYPLAYERS** whisper hurriedly behind their backs.)*

ALBERT. *(Sotto voce, to **FRED**.)* It's going to be one of her own stories, by the look of it...

BETHANY. Be extra careful...

FRED. Anything special I should look out for?

JENKIN. Everything.

TALITHA. Remember her name—Great Aunt Repetitus. That means her stories tend to go round in circles...

NELL. Sometimes they do.

BETHANY. But not always...

FRED. *(Bewildered.)* Is that good?

ALBERT. It can be...

JENKIN. But not always...

FRED. *(Sarcastically.)* Oh, thanks. That's a lot of help.

*(The **STORYTELLERS** have reached their respective positions.)*

G-AUNT R. Pay attention. This is a story of The Enchanted Farmer's Sons.

ALBERT. *(Whispering.)* I don't know that one...

BETHANY. No...

G-AUNT R. *(Sharply.)* Then you'd better listen then, hadn't you, Albert?

ALBERT. *(Nervously.)* Oh, yes...

G-AUNT R. You know what happens to people who don't listen, don't you, Albert?

ALBERT. Oh, yes.

G-AUNT R. Something awful happens to them in Chapter Two, doesn't it, Albert?

ALBERT. Yes, yes. I'm listening.

G-AUNT R. Good. Then I shall begin. There was once a rich farmer...

(**ALBERT** *dives at once into his bag for the appropriate headgear, etc. He finds, and puts on, his woodcutter's hat and picks out an axe during the following.*)

...who owned a great deal of land. And the land was so rich that his crops flourished and his cattle grew big and fat... *(Impatiently.)* I said a farmer, Albert, a farmer not a woodcutter.

ALBERT. *(Nervously.)* Sorry. Just a second.

(*He dives back in his bag again for a fresh disguise and equips himself with appropriate farmer's gear during the following.*)

G-AUNT R. You're not even going to last through Chapter One at this rate, are you, Albert? The farmer's rich land was bounded on one side by a wide river and on the other by a thick wood. And in this wood, so people said, lived a wicked witch—but nobody had ever seen her—and she never bothered anyone, not at all. Now with the farmer—that's better, Albert—lived the farmer's wife...

(**TALITHA** *immediately dons an apron and stands next to* **ALBERT**.)

A cheerful, good-natured woman who worked hard alongside her husband and bore him two fine twin sons, Jethro...

(**JENKIN** *steps forward to join the group.*)

...and Jonas...

(**FRED** *steps forward to join the group.*)

And because they were rich and food was plentiful and their parents happy and easy-going, the two boys grew up big and strong and were a credit to their parents. They worked alongside their father in the fields and because all of them worked so hard the farm prospered and their happiness increased day by day.

(*Jolly scenes at the farm from the four concerned.*)

They were all quite content in each other's company. Which was fortunate since their nearest neighbour, another farmer, lived several miles away, further along the river valley. Though sometimes his daughter Molly would pass by on her way to market. Whenever she did, she would always smile and wave to them.

(**NELL** *passes by, smiling and waving.*)

NELL. Morning, all.

OTHERS. (*Equally.*) Morning, Molly.

G-AUNT R. And so it continued, year after year, until the sons had grown to manhood and the farmer and his wife were no longer quite as young as they had been. And then one year, on the boys' seventeenth birthday, the family were celebrating as usual when there was a terrible storm...

(**KEVIN** *supplies the thunder and rain.*)

And the storm wasn't just an ordinary storm but continued for days on end. And the fields became flooded and the crops were ruined and finally the river burst its banks and many of their cattle were swept away...

(*Cattle noises above the storm from* **KEVIN**.)

...despite every attempt to save them. And the waters continued to rise and soon even their home was flooded and for several days the family had to sit on their roof, hoping the river would get no higher or they would all be drowned without a doubt. And when finally the storm stopped...and the river went down...

(*There is a gurgling noise and then the rain effects cease.*)

...and the poor family finally came down off the roof, they found they'd lost everything. They were no longer rich at all but quite poor. And they sat and stared at the damage and destruction and felt very sad indeed.

(*The family sit, gloomily.*)

Just then, a stranger came riding by, a dark eyed woman on a jet black stallion...

(KEVIN produces stallion noises as BETHANY rides up.)

BETHANY. Whooa, there, Cyanide!

G-AUNT R. She was elegant and beautiful and looked, at the very least, like a royal princess or even a queen. But she was neither of these. She was, in fact, the wicked witch from the thick, dark wood. All these many years she had lived alone weaving her spells and mixing her potions but lately she had begun to feel lonely. For she realized that even witches grew old, though they live much longer than we do—she was now four hundred and fifty—and that she wanted companionship. For though she had married—several times—she had grown tired of all her husbands over the years and had got rid of them all—either by poisoning them or eating them. Moreover, none of them had lived long enough to give her the child she so wanted. And lately over the last few days she had found herself weeping bitterly—indeed it was her tears that had caused the rain to fall and the river to rise. But now she had stopped crying, she had decided to seek out a new husband. Someone young and strong and handsome. And as she rode past the farm she spied Jethro and Jonas. And although she could not immediately choose between them she knew her search was over. She wanted one of them for her own. And she determined somehow she would have him, by fair means or foul.

(BETHANY hisses to herself. Her horse whinnies, courtesy of KEVIN.)

But the witch was cunning and she decided first to try and trick them.

BETHANY. Hallo, there...

ALBERT. Afternoon.

TALITHA. Afternoon.

JENKIN. 'Noon.

FRED. 'Noon.

BETHANY. Golly! What a mess! Poor old you!

ALBERT. Ay.

TALITHA. Ay.

JENKIN. Ay.

FRED. Ay.

BETHANY. Lot of clearing up for you to do.

ALBERT. Happen there will be.

TALITHA. Ay.

JENKIN. Ay.

FRED. Happen.

BETHANY. Anything I can do to help?

(They all look at her.)

If I can help in any way at all...?

*(**ALBERT**, **TALITHA**, **JENKIN** and **FRED**, in turn, grunt negatively.)*

(Doubtfully.) Yes. Look—er—I'm—I do know a bit of magic...

ALBERT. Magic?

BETHANY. Just a teeny-weeny bit...

TALITHA. *(Doubtfully.)* Well...

BETHANY. I mean, it's white magic—it's perfectly harmless, I promise you...

ALBERT. *(Suspiciously.)* Oh, ay?

BETHANY. Oh, yes. I do assure you of that. I would never—no—not at all. It's just—well, you've got the most frightful job on your hands otherwise, haven't you? I mean just clearing the place up. It could take years.

TALITHA. *(Unhappily.)* Ay. Reckon it could.

BETHANY. I mean, even with your two fine strapping boys to help you. What are their names, may I ask?

TALITHA. This one's Jethro...

JENKIN. How dy'do.

TALITHA. And this is Jonas.

FRED. How'do.

TALITHA. Jonas is half a minute younger than Jethro.

BETHANY. You must be very proud of them both.

TALITHA. Oh, we are.

BETHANY. *(Smiling at* TALITHA.*)* I really must congratulate you. Glorious boys. They're a credit to you.

TALITHA. Thank you very much.

BETHANY. Well, I must be getting along... *(She makes as if to remount her horse.)*

TALITHA. Just a moment... 'Scuse me...

BETHANY. Yes?

TALITHA. What's... What about this magic, then?

ALBERT. Now, Mother…

TALITHA. I'm only asking…

ALBERT. You don't want to be doing with all that…

TALITHA. I'm only asking her, that's all. I'm only asking. No harm in asking.

ALBERT. Well…

TALITHA. What about it, then?

BETHANY. Oh. Well, it's quite simple. All you'll need to do is to cut the heart and liver from one of your dead cattle…

TALITHA. Heart and liver, yes…

BETHANY. Then mince it well and then crush it with some fresh elderberries—or if you can't get elderberries, juniper berries will do the trick just as well—

TALITHA. Juniper berries, yes…

BETHANY. Leave that to marinate in a small earthenware pot or basin.

TALITHA. Pot or basin, yes…

BETHANY. Then in a couple of hours, all you do is add the ears from a dead vole and four tablespoonsful of common or garden black treacle. Yes?

TALITHA. Vole…black treacle, right.

BETHANY. Then bury that, in the bowl, at midnight, under a holly bush. Female bush, remember. With berries. Not male. Very important, that. OK? Got that?

TALITHA. Yes. Got that.

ALBERT. Sounds a load of mumbo to me.

BETHANY. Yes, doesn't it just? But mock ye not. More often than not, you'd be amazed, it actually works. Give it a try.

TALITHA. I will. Thank you.

BETHANY. *(Mounting her steed.)* Cheerio, then. I may pop back—easy, Cyanide, boy! —see how you got on! Byee!

(**BETHANY** *gallops away,* **KEVIN** *providing a whinny and the sound of hooves.*)

(The others stare after her.)

ALBERT. Bye.

TALITHA. Bye.

JENKIN. Bye.

FRED. Bye.

(A pause.)

TALITHA. Nice woman. I think I might give all that a try…

ALBERT. Oh no, you won't.

TALITHA. Why not? Where's the harm?

ALBERT. Because it's magic. That's where's the harm.

TALITHA. White magic. You heard her. White magic.

ALBERT. White magic. Black magic. Magic's magic and no good came of anyone who touched it. You start on any of that, I'll lock you in the pig pen, all right?

TALITHA. *(Sulkily.)* All right.

G-AUNT R. And so, despite the mother's protests, the family set about cleaning up by hand. But once they'd cleaned they realized they'd then have to plough and replant and restock the farm. And that would all take years and years and years. But nobody dared mention the magic. Because nobody particularly wanted to spend the night in the pig pen. And when it grew dark -

(There is an owl noise from **KEVIN**.*)*

G-AUNT R. - because they were all so tired they went to bed early. But the mother lay awake and as soon as the others were asleep, she crept downstairs and set about finding the ingredients for the witch's magic spell. Luckily they had a juniper bush and she found a drowned vole just round the back of the house— and she buried the bowl under a nearby holly tree. Then, having followed the witch's instructions to the letter, she crept back to bed. And the following morning, at dawn -

(There is a cock crow from **KEVIN**.*)*

- they all arose and looked out of the window:

ALBERT. Well!

TALITHA. Oh!

JENKIN. Cor!

FRED. Lumme!

G-AUNT R. The place was transformed. Where once there'd been mud and dead animals, contented cattle were grazing on rich green grass...

(There are cow noises from **KEVIN**.*)*

Chickens were foraging...

*(***KEVIN** *adds chicken noises.)*

Lambs were leaping...

(**KEVIN** *adds sheep noises.*)

Pigs were rooting...

(**KEVIN** *adds pig noises.*)

And the whole farmyard was a hive of activity.

(**KEVIN** *adds full barnyard cacophony for a second or so, then fades the sounds under the following dialogue.*)

ALBERT. This any of your doing, Mother?

TALITHA. Me? Now would I?

ALBERT. You! You ought to be in that pig pen, you ought, woman.

(*He stares at her for a moment Then he smiles. She smiles at him. The two boys smile, too.*)

(*With a great whoop.*) Yeehaw!

TALITHA. Yayho!

JENKIN. Yahoo!

FRED. Yessirreee!

(*They do a swift barn dance. They collapse happily.*)

(**NELL** *enters.*)

G-AUNT R. ...and young Molly, passing on her way to market, stared at them all in amazement...

NELL. Morning.

OTHERS. Morning, Molly.

NELL. *(More intimately.)* Morning, Jethro.

JENKIN. How d'you do.

NELL. *(More warmly still.)* Morning, Jonas.

FRED. *(Awkwardly.)* 'Llo, then.

NELL. *(Softly and urgently.)* Be careful, Flavius.

FRED. What?

NELL. Careful…

FRED. Why, what's—?

(Before she can say more, **GREAT AUNT REPETITUS** *looks at them suspiciously.* **NELL** *hastily draws back.)*

G-AUNT R. *(Firmly continuing.)* And young Molly continued on happily to market.

*(***NELL** *moves away, reluctantly.)*

JENKIN. *(To* **FRED.***)* She's after you.

FRED. What?

JENKIN. That Molly. She fancies you a' all.

FRED. *(Scornfully.)* Nar. *(He stares after* **NELL.***)* Reckon so?

JENKIN. Reckon.

G-AUNT R. And so life on the farm was back to normal. Or nearly back to normal. For as the farmer so wisely pointed out, once you have dabbled in magic of any kind, life can never really be back to normal again. And as we shall see, this family now found themselves in debt to a witch. A few days later she returned.

(A whinny and sound of horse's hooves as before.)

*(**BETHANY** gallops into view.)*

BETHANY. *(Cheerfully.)* Whooaaa, Cyanide! Hallo, there!

ALBERT. *(Equally cheerful.)* Afternoon!

TALITHA. Afternoon!

JENKIN. Afternoon!

FRED. Afternoon!

BETHANY. I see it worked. The recipe. It worked.

ALBERT. Oh, ay, we reckoned to give it a try. The wife here was against it but…

BETHANY. Splendid!

TALITHA. Thank you very much. Say thank you to the lady, boys.

JENKIN. Ta!

FRED. Ta!

BETHANY. Magnificent boys! Bigger than ever. Well, see you around sometime, I expect. Yup, Cyanide! Byeee!

*(**BETHANY** gallops away as before.)*

(The others stare after her.)

ALBERT. Bye.

TALITHA. Bye.

JENKIN. Bye.

FRED. Bye.

(Pause.)

TALITHA. Nice woman.

ALBERT. Very pleasant.

JENKIN. She's a looker an' all!

FRED. *(Smirking.)* Ay.

TALITHA. That's enough of that, you two! None of that smuttin' around here, right? Or your dad'll put you both in the pig pen. Right, Dad?

ALBERT. Right. Back to work, then.

JENKIN. *(As they go about their tasks, to* **FRED.***)* I wouldn't mind getting with her in a pig pen.

*(***FRED** *sniggers.)*

G-AUNT R. And, for a few months, life continued happily as before on the farm. Winter ended, spring came and went and then came summer and day after day of glorious sunshine. At first the family welcomed the sun. But the days got hotter still and the wide river began to shrink in its bed until finally it dried up to a trickle of mud. And suddenly as the animals started to grow thirsty and die, the sun was no longer a friend but a foe that had brought the farmer's most feared enemy of all—drought. Little did the family know that all this was caused not by the sun but by the increasing heat of the witch's lust. It was so hot, even at night—especially at night—that no living creature wanted to move.

(The family sit on the ground, panting in the heat.)

ALBERT. *(Speaking with difficulty.)* How much water we got left?

TALITHA. Just till tomorrow. Then we're dry, that's it.

JENKIN. What we going to do? We can't not drink. What we going to do then?

FRED. We got to drink, haven't we? What we going to do?

TALITHA. Dad?

ALBERT. I don't know. I don't know.

(The sound of galloping hooves and the whinny of a horse.)

*(***BETHANY*** rides into view.)*

BETHANY. Hallo there! Isn't it glorious? Another scorching day. Whoaa there, Cyanide! Easy, boy. What weather! How long can it last? That's what we'd all like to know, eh?

ALBERT. *(Grimly.)* We would.

TALITHA. Ay.

JENKIN. Right.

FRED. Ar.

BETHANY. Oh dear. Problems?

ALBERT. *(Indicating.)* Problems? Look at it.

BETHANY. Oh, yes. Oh, dear. Why are all your cattle lying down? Are they having a nap?

ALBERT. They're dead, aren't they?

BETHANY. Dead?

TALITHA. Drought.

BETHANY. Oh, dear. One just doesn't realize. Living alone. Of course, I have a private well so I'm laughing. Oh dear. Look, I don't know if I can help at all but—I do know a recipe that might—I repeat might—just work…

TALITHA. Recipe?

ALBERT. More magic?

BETHANY. *Sort* of magic, yes. Very, very, very mild though.

ALBERT. *(Doubtfully.)* Well…

TALITHA. What is it?

BETHANY. Well—you all have to do this together—if it's going to work… All right?

ALBERT. Maybe. Yes.

BETHANY. It won't work otherwise. It sounds a bit silly but—have you any nails or sharp tin tacks in the house…?

ALBERT. Yes, we got a few of them.

BETHANY. Good. Now, you sprinkle some of them about an inch deep into four large bowls, all right?

TALITHA. Four large bowls, right.

BETHANY. Then, at the time you'd normally go to bed, you each stand barefoot in one of the bowls, OK?

TALITHA. Barefoot?

ALBERT. On the tin tacks?

BETHANY. Yes. With a pillow case over your head.

TALITHA. …pillow case…

BETHANY. And then—here's the tricky bit—you must all say together:

A rabbit cannot whistle Strauss,

Picasso couldn't paint a mouse,

But may it rain upon this house.

Have you all got that? All together:

ALL. *(Except* **BETHANY.***)* A rabbit cannot whistle Strauss,

Picasso couldn't paint a mouse,

But may it rain upon this house.

BETHANY. Splendid.

ALBERT. How many times do we have to say that?

BETHANY. Just until the cock crows.

JENKIN. All night?

FRED. Flippin' heck!

TALITHA. Now, now! Language!

BETHANY. Sorry. It doesn't sound like a load of fun—but if all else fails—you might like to try it. Mouth-watering boys! Must dash now, sorry. Byee!

(**BETHANY** *leaps astride her steed. She gallops away with noises, as before.*)

(*The others stare after her.*)

ALBERT. Bye.

TALITHA. Bye.

JENKIN. Bye.

FRED. Bye.

(*There is a pause.*)

TALITHA. Well, I'm afraid I'm not doing that. Standing in a bowl of tin tacks all night with a bag on my head, chanting. Not for no-one, I'm sorry.

JENKIN. Nor me.

FRED. Nor me.

(They look at **ALBERT.***)*

TALITHA. Dad?

ALBERT. *(Less certainly.)* Oh, no. Nor me.

G-AUNT R. And so that night, they all decided to ignore the witch's advice, since none of them fancied standing in a bowl all night with a bag on their head chanting. So they lay down in bed and tried to sleep. But the father, as soon as he thought all the others were asleep, crept downstairs on his own with his pillowcase. After all there was no harm in trying. And maybe the magic would work with just him on his own.

ALBERT. Happen it might.

G-AUNT R. He took off his shoes and socks and, having filled a kitchen bowl with tin tacks, stood in it barefoot.

*(***ALBERT** *produces a bowl from his bag and a pillow case. He stands in the bowl.)*

ALBERT. Oooh! Aaaa! Eeee! *(He pulls the pillow case over his head and mutters the witch's incantation under the next.)*

A rabbit cannot whistle Strauss,

Picasso couldn't paint a mouse,

But may it rain upon this house, *etc.*

G-AUNT R. And soon the mother had also crept downstairs with her pillowcase...

(**TALITHA** *creeps down and repeats* **ALBERT***'s business.*)

TALITHA. *(As she stands in her bowl.)* Ooo! Aaa! Eee! *(She puts her pillowcase over her head.)*

A rabbit cannot whistle Strauss,

Picasso couldn't paint a mouse,

But may it rain upon this house, *etc.*

(**JENKIN** *and* **FRED** *in turn do the same until they are all standing in bowls with pillowcases on their heads and chanting.*)

G-AUNT R. And so they continued all night. Of course, if they had only known, what they were doing wasn't magic at all. No real witch would ever give away her spells to ordinary mortals. And even as they stood there chanting all through the night, the witch watched them from her castle deep in the wood and laughed and laughed...

(**BETHANY** *cackles.*)

But she also did a little real magic of her own so that in the morning, as soon as the cock crew...

(*A cock crow from* **KEVIN** *followed by a clap of thunder and rain. The family stop chanting.*)

ALBERT. *(Removing his pillowcase.)* Rain!

(He sees the others.)

Oh!

TALITHA. *(Doing likewise.)* Rain!

(She sees the boys)

TALITHA. Oh!

JENKIN. *(Doing likewise.)* Rain! *(He sees* **FRED.***)* Oh!

FRED. *(Doing likewise.)* Rain! It worked!

ALBERT. *(With a great whoop.)* Yeehaw!

TALITHA. Yayho!

JENKIN. Yahoo!

FRED. Yessirreee!

(They do a swift barn dance. They collapse happily.)

*(***NELL*** enters.)*

G-AUNT R. And young Molly who was passing on her way to market stared at them all in amazement...

NELL. Morning.

OTHERS. Morning, Molly.

NELL. *(Very warmly.)* Morning, Jonas.

FRED. *(Awkwardly.)* 'Llo, then.

NELL. *(Softly and urgently.)* Be careful, Flavius.

FRED. What?

NELL. Careful...

FRED. Why, what's—?

(Again, before she can say more, **GREAT AUNT REPETITUS** *looks over suspiciously.* **NELL** *hastily draws back.)*

G-AUNT R. *(Firmly continuing.)* And young Molly continued on happily to market.

*(**NELL** moves away, reluctantly.)*

JENKIN. *(To **FRED**.)* Whey-hey!

FRED. Gerroff!

G-AUNT R. And so life on the farm was back to normal. Or nearly back to normal. For as I have said before, once you have had dealings with witches, however slight, life can never really get back to normal again.

(A whinny and sound of horse's hooves as before. **BETHANY** *gallops into view.)*

BETHANY. *(Cheerfully.)* Hallo, there! Whoaaa, Cyanide!

ALBERT. *(Equally cheerfully.)* Afternoon!

TALITHA. Afternoon!

JENKIN. Afternoon!

FRED. Afternoon!

BETHANY. I see it worked. My little tip. It worked.

ALBERT. Oh, ay, the wife reckoned to give it a try. I was dead against it but...

BETHANY. Splendid.

TALITHA. Thank you very much. Say thank you to the lady, boys.

JENKIN. Ta!

FRED. Ta!

BETHANY. Pulse-racing boys! Well, see you around sometime, I expect. Byeee! *(She moves to exit.)*

TALITHA. Er—excuse me...

BETHANY. Steady, Cyanide. Hallo?

TALITHA. Would—would you care to have a spot of supper with us sometime? If you've a moment? Just to say thank you, like. We was wondering if you would, weren't we, Dad?

ALBERT. Were we?

TALITHA. We were.

BETHANY. Oh, how sweet of you. I'd love to. When would suit?

TALITHA. Well, any time really. We aren't going anywhere.

BETHANY. Tomorrow night any good?

TALITHA. Oh, yes, tomorrow would be perfect.

BETHANY. Super! Look forward to it. Byee! Yup, Cyanide!

(**BETHANY** *gallops off, as before.*)

ALBERT. Bye.

TALITHA. Bye.

JENKIN. Bye.

FRED. Bye.

(*A pause.*)

ALBERT. What you want to go and do that for?

TALITHA. What?

ALBERT. Ask her to supper.

TALITHA. Why not?

ALBERT. She's a lady. She don't want to eat supper with us.

TALITHA. She's also a very nice woman and I like her. So there. She's also done us a good turn—two good turns and we ain't done her any, so we owe her. And she's coming and that's final, all right?

(**TALITHA** *stamps indoors. The three men look at each other.*)

ALBERT. Well, then. You'd better comb your hair then, you two, hadn't you?

G-AUNT R. Next day, they all worked hard to make the place neat and tidy. The boys helped their mother in the kitchen whilst she prepared the most splendid supper she could. When they had finished, they waited anxiously for their guest to arrive. Alas, if only they had known who their guest really was. For if there is one thing worse than accepting favours from witches, it is allowing them into your home to sit at your table.

(*The family stand round the table.*)

TALITHA. Think it looks all right?

ALBERT. Looks good to me, Mother. Eh, lads?

JENKIN. Yes.

FRED. Yes. Can we start, then?

TALITHA. No, you can't. You wait for your guest.

JENKIN. Where is she then? Gone half-past.

(**KEVIN** *produces the sound of the horse as* **BETHANY** *appears. She clutches a bottle.*)

ALBERT. This'll be her.

BETHANY. Whoaa there, Cyanide! Good boy! Hallo there.

ALBERT. Evenin'.

TALITHA. Evenin'.

JENKIN. Evenin'.

FRED. Evenin'.

BETHANY. I hope it's all right, I brought a bottle of vino. That OK?

ALBERT. Vino? I don't think we've tried it. What is it?

BETHANY. Wine.

TALITHA. Oh, wine!

BETHANY. Help! You're not teetotal by some ghastly chance?

ALBERT. Oh, no, we're partial to a drop of wine.

BETHANY. Super! I hope the boys will be allowed some?

TALITHA. Just a drop. We don't encourage it.

JENKIN. Oh, Mum.

G-AUNT R. And so they all sat down to supper. And the witch had the farmer open her bottle of wine and then insisted that they all drink a toast.

BETHANY. Now listen, everyone. Before we eat. I want to drink one toast, OK?

ALBERT. Right.

BETHANY. To us all. To new-found friends.

ALL. New-found friends.

(They all drink.)

G-AUNT R. The meal was a great success. The witch knew dozens of very funny stories—some of them a little bit risqué, I'm afraid—but she kept them amused all through the meal. Maybe some of the merriment was due to the wine which seemed, it has to be said, rather strong. At last it was time for the witch to leave.

BETHANY. Well, thank you again. This has been terrific.

ALBERT. No, no...

TALITHA. No, thank *you*.

BETHANY. You're just dear people, all of you. *(She turns to the boys.)* And as for you two, I want to wrap you both up and take you home with me, I really do. *(She laughs.)*

(They all laugh.)

JENKIN. Wouldn't mind that myself...

TALITHA. Now, now... You wouldn't want them for long, I can tell you...

BETHANY. I don't know which is the more handsome, do you? Which would you say, Mother?

TALITHA. Neither of 'em. They're both as ugly as sin, if you ask me.

BETHANY. Hark at her! Hark at her! Pay no attention to her, boys, do you hear?

(She hugs them both in turn, rather lingeringly, during the following.)

BETHANY. And remember this, boys. Sin doesn't unnecessarily have to be ugly, either. Believe me, it can sometimes be very, very beautiful. Sleep tight, little heartwrenchers.

(She moves to her horse and remounts.)

Good-night, all. Easy, Cyanide! Night then! Night!

*(**BETHANY** gallops away, as before.)*

ALBERT. Night.

TALITHA. Night.

JENKIN. Night.

FRED. Night.

(A pause.)

TALITHA. A real nice woman.

JENKIN. *(Gazing after her with some desire.)* Yes. Real nice...

FRED. *(Likewise.)* Real, real nice...

ALBERT. That wine was a bit of all right.

G-AUNT R. But it wasn't really. For, as you may have guessed, the witch's wine was actually a magic potion with many powers. The mixture had no effect on the witch herself— she had made sure it wouldn't—but it did strange things to the family. Like all wine, only more so, it was half a love potion and half a poison. And so it was that their sleep was filled with weird dreams.

*(Dream music from **KEVIN**.)*

For Jethro and Jonas, it seemed that the witch visited them both looking more beautiful and desirable than ever.

(**BETHANY** *appears. During the following she beckons to* **JENKIN** *and* **FRED**, *who arise dreamlike from their beds and move to her.*)

For the witch couldn't yet decide which one she should choose to love her for ever. She wanted them both equally...

(**BETHANY** *kisses* **JENKIN** *and* **FRED** *in turn on their foreheads.*)

But she knew that finally the choice would be hers alone. Whichever of them she wanted she need only kiss his forehead and he would be hers for ever after.

(*During the following* **BETHANY** *takes* **JENKIN**'s *and* **FRED**'s *hands and whirls them round her as if trying to choose between them.*)

Meanwhile, their parents were having a much less enjoyable dream...

(**ALBERT** *and* **TALITHA** *sit up and produce two large foam rubber mallets from their bags. Each starts to batter him- or herself on the head for a bit.* **KEVIN** *provides percussive accompaniment.*)

ALBERT
TALITHA } (*Together.*) Ooo! Ow! Ooo! Ow! *etc.*

G-AUNT R. Until at last all of them, for one reason or another, were quite exhausted.

(*They all return to their beds exhausted.*)

(**BETHANY** *withdraws.*)

G-AUNT R. Came the dawn...

(**KEVIN** *gives a cock-crow.*)

ALBERT. (*Sitting up, groaning.*) Ooo! My head...

TALITHA. (*Likewise.*) Aaaaaah!

(*They both stagger downstairs.*)

ALBERT. I think I'm dying.

TALITHA. So am I...

G-AUNT R. The brothers, on the other hand, seemed to have suffered no ill effects...

JENKIN. (*Sitting up with a smile.*) Oh!

FRED. (*Likewise.*) Ah!

G-AUNT R. Unless you call being hopelessly in love an ill effect...

JENKIN. (*To himself.*) I love her...

FRED. (*To himself.*) I love her...

JENKIN. (*To himself.*) For ever...

FRED. (*To himself.*) And ever...

(*They both get up and, passing their parents, go outside.*)

ALBERT. Morning, Jethro...

TALITHA. Morning, Jonas...

G-AUNT R. But the boys had eyes now for one and only one...

ALBERT. What's up with those two, then?

TALITHA. Search me. Want your breakfast? Bacon and eggs?

ALBERT. *(Feeling sick.)* No, I don't.

G-AUNT R. And the brothers stood in the field and dreamt of the woman they both loved—though as yet, neither knew that they both loved the same woman. But when Molly came by on her way to town...

*(*NELL *passes by.)*

NELL. Morning. *(She smiles at* **FRED***.)* Morning, Jonas.

G-AUNT R. Neither noticed her at all...

NELL. Jonas... Jonas... It's me. *(Softer.)* Flavius! Flavius! *(Urgently.)* Flavius...

FRED. *(Impatiently.)* What? What is it...

NELL. Flavius...

FRED. Go away.

NELL. Flavius, I...

G-AUNT R. Stop!

(The **PLAYERS** *freeze.)*

What are you doing there, child?

NELL. Nothing, Great Aunt.

G-AUNT R. Yes, you are. You keep doing it, I've been watching you. You behave as you're told, all right?

NELL. Yes, Great Aunt.

G-AUNT R. *(Studying her.)* Yes. I think something nasty could well happen to you in the next chapter.

NELL. Oh no, I...

G-AUNT R. *(Firmly continuing.)* And young Molly continued unhappily to market. Unaware of the events that lay ahead.

(**NELL** *moves away reluctantly.*)

JENKIN. What's up with you, then?

FRED. What?

JENKIN. Don't you say good-morning to her any more then, your lover girl?

FRED. She's not my lover girl.

JENKIN. Course she is.

FRED. Not any more. Somebody else now, isn't there?

JENKIN. Who?

FRED. Her. Who else. Her from last night. That's who. She's the one now.

JENKIN. Oh no, she's not. She's mine that one.

FRED. Yours?

JENKIN. Mine.

FRED. She's not, you know.

JENKIN. She is, you know.

FRED. Oh yes?

JENKIN. Yes.

FRED. Over my dead body.

JENKIN. If necessary.

FRED. Right.

JENKIN. Right.

(They start to fight, rolling on the ground. **ALBERT** *and* **TALITHA** *come out to discover them.)*

ALBERT. What's happening here...?

TALITHA. What's going on?

ALBERT. Jethro...

TALITHA. Jonas! Stop it both of you. They've never fought like this before. Never. What's happened to them, Father?

ALBERT. I don't know. I don't know. It's like the devil's in them.

*(***ALBERT** *and* **TALITHA** *try vainly to separate the two fighters.)*

G-AUNT R. It was indeed the devil in them both. And—talk of the devil—

*(***BETHANY** *comes riding up, with effects, as before, from* **KEVIN.***)*

BETHANY. Whooaa! Whoaa there, Cyanide! Morning. What's all the ballyhoo?

TALITHA. Oh, my lady, stop them. Please, please stop them... Before they kill each other.

BETHANY. *(Firmly.)* Jethro! Jonas! Stop! Please...

(The brothers stop immediately. They sit on the ground, staring up at **BETHANY** *in adoration.)*

JENKIN. Oh!

FRED. Oh!

BETHANY. That's better. You bad, bad boys. Now what's the trouble? Tell me the problem.

JENKIN. I love you.

TALITHA. Jethro!

FRED. So do I.

TALITHA. Jonas!

JENKIN. Desperately!

FRED. Passionately!

ALBERT. Beg pardon, Miss. I'll lock them both in the pig pen. That'll cool 'em.

BETHANY. No, no... Please, not on my account.

TALITHA. You daft pair. You can't love her. What are you saying? She don't want you, does she?

BETHANY. *(Swiftly.)* Oh, but I do, I do, I do. *(She recovers.)* I mean I might. I could. Given time. Perhaps. Possibly. Who can tell with a woman's heart?

JENKIN. You could love me?

FRED. Or me?

BETHANY. Oh, yes. Quite possibly.

JENKIN. Oh.

FRED. Oh.

ALBERT. Well...

TALITHA. Well, that's very nice of you, I'm sure...

BETHANY. But which one of you, that's the problem.

JENKIN. Better be me, hadn't it?

FRED. Has to be me, hasn't it?

JENKIN. Gerroff! *(He threatens* **FRED.***)*

FRED. Gerroff! *(He threatens* **JENKIN.***)*

BETHANY. Now, now, boys. May I suggest something? *(To* **TALITHA.***)* May I borrow them from you for three days?

TALITHA. Three days?

BETHANY. To stay with me whilst I decide? I promise you, at the end of three days, one of them will be returned to you. As good as new.

ALBERT. Well, I suppose three days…

TALITHA. No longer…

ALBERT. There's the harvest…

TALITHA. And the animals…

BETHANY. Three days is all I need. I promise.

ALBERT. Right.

TALITHA. Right.

BETHANY. Happy, boys?

JENKIN. 'Spose.

FRED. 'Spose.

BETHANY. Then away we go. Yup there, Cyanide.

G-AUNT R. And so the two brothers went with the witch deep into the forest, walking each side of her huge black stallion. As they reached the edge of the dark wood, they turned and waved to their parents—and despite their love for the witch, they both felt sudden sadness for they knew that only one of them would ever return again to the sunshine. The forest was darker than they could possibly have imagined. And although they were both grown men, they were rather glad to have company with them. The witch, on the other hand, seemed quite at home in the wood. As she rode along she sang softly to herself...

BETHANY. *(Singing.)*
AS LOUD AS YOU SCREAM, AS MUCH AS YOU SHOUT,
ONCE YOU'RE IN HERE, YOU WILL NEVER GET OUT,
WITHOUT ANY DOUBT, YOU WILL NEVER GET OUT,
NEVER GET OUT, NEVER GET OUT...

G-AUNT R. And the brothers joined in...

JENKIN. *(Singing with her.)*
FRED. NEVER GET OUT, NEVER GET OUT—

G-AUNT R. Finally they arrived at the very darkest part of the forest and there—before them huge and lowering and dripping with green slime—stood the witch's castle itself.

*(A chord from **KEVIN**.)*

And before the brothers could say anything, the witch led them inside and straight to their room.

*(**KEVIN** makes a dripping water sound.)*

BETHANY. Here we are boys, you don't mind sharing, do you? Make yourselves comfortable. Dinner's at eight.

*(**KEVIN** plays a huge door slam.)*

*(**BETHANY** leaves them.)*

FRED. *(Nervously.)* It's very dark, isn't it?

JENKIN. *(Likewise.)* I can't find the light switch.

FRED. It's a funny sort of bedroom. I can't find a bed.

(**JENKIN** *tries the door.* **KEVIN** *makes a door handle rattling sound.*)

JENKIN. The door's locked. She's locked us in…

FRED. It's more like a dungeon…

JENKIN. The roof s leaking.

G-AUNT R. The brothers stood in the dark for hours—for they couldn't even find anywhere to sit down and the floor was very damp. Secretly they both wished they were back home in their snug, dry farmhouse—but it was too late now… Far too late.

(*A door opening sound from* **KEVIN.**)

(**BETHANY** *reappears.*)

BETHANY. Come on, boys. Dinner time.

(*She moves off again.*)

G-AUNT R. And the brothers came blinking into the light and, after a little searching, found their way to the castle dining-room.

(**KEVIN** *plays some witch's dining-room music.*)

BETHANY. Oh, there you are. Come in. Sit down. Shame you didn't bother to dress for dinner.

JENKIN. We couldn't find the light…

BETHANY. The light?

JENKIN. To see anything.

BETHANY. Light. You don't need light. Not here, I promise you. Once you've lived here for a little while you'll be able to see in the dark. Like everything and everyone that lives around here.

(A trumpeting sound of some strange beast echoes along the corridors. The brothers jump in alarm.)

*(***NELL.*** enters in an apron carrying a serving dish. She appears to have been crying. She serves the meal.)*

Ah, now. I think you know my new little maid, don't you? You both know Molly?

FRED. Molly!

BETHANY. Yes, Jonas. You remember Molly, I'm sure. She's just joined the staff here. She was a little unhappy to start with, but she's settling in nicely now, aren't you, Molly?

*(***NELL*** does not reply but continues serving.)*

(Sharply.) Aren't you, girl?

NELL. *(Jumping.)* Yes, Madam.

(The background muzak takes a turn for the worse.)

BETHANY. Oh, I adore this tune... *(She closes her eyes.)*

NELL. *(Whispering.)* Flavius... Flavius...

FRED. *(Seeming not to understand.)* Flavius...

NELL. You're in terrible danger...

FRED. *(Still bemused.)* What?

NELL. Flavius!

FRED. *(Loudly.)* What?

BETHANY. *(Opening her eyes.)* What?

FRED. Nothing.

BETHANY. Get back to the kitchen, Molly.

NELL. Yes, Madam.

BETHANY. And clean the floor in there, it's filthy.

NELL. There's no mop, madam.

BETHANY. Then lick it, girl. Lick it. What do you think your tongue's for?

NELL. Yes, madam.

(NELL moves away.)

BETHANY. Eat up, boys. You must both be starving. I like my men big and strong. Eat up…

JENKIN. *(Unhappily.)* I don't reckon I'm that hungry—

BETHANY. *(Savagely.)* Eat it!

JENKIN. Right.

FRED. Right.

(The two men start eating.)

JENKIN. *(After a mouthful.)* Ugghhh!

FRED. *(Likewise.)* Ugggh!

BETHANY. Nice?

JENKIN. What is it?

BETHANY. Secret recipe.

JENKIN. Oh.

(*They both take another tentative mouthful.*)

BETHANY. But I will tell you it was only freshly killed.

FRED. Grug!

JENKIN. Grew!

BETHANY. You're not vegetarians, are you?

JENKIN. No.

FRED. No.

BETHANY. Only I don't like vegetarians. Do you know what I do to vegetarians?

JENKIN. No?

BETHANY. I dig a hole and plant them. Headfirst.

FRED. Ah.

BETHANY. (*Smiling at them.*) Do you know, I have actually come to a decision already. Which of you it is who's going to stay here with me. Isn't that exciting?

JENKIN. (*Dully.*) Yes.

BETHANY. I'll tell you both after dinner, shall I?

FRED. Yes.

BETHANY. Aren't you both dying to know who I've chosen?

(*No reply.*)

(*Sharply.*) Aren't you?

JENKIN.
FRED. } (*Together.*) Yes!

G-AUNT R. Suddenly, despite the fact that the dinner tasted quite, quite disgusting, the brothers lingered over the food as long as possible, savouring every mouthful—for neither wanted the meal to end. But finally, even bad things come to an end.

(**NELL** *returns.*)

BETHANY. Clear away, Molly. And then bring us some wine. We have a toast to make to the lucky winner.

NELL. Yes, Madam. (*She looks despairingly at* **FRED**.)

(*During the next,* **NELL** *removes the plates and returns at once with the wine.*)

BETHANY. Up you get, boys, and stand over there.

(**FRED** *and* **JENKIN** *obey her.*)

(*Surveying them.*) Now, let me take one last look. (*She surveys them from all angles.*)

JENKIN. (*To* **FRED**.) I don't mind—if you'd rather stay—I don't mind leaving at all...

FRED. No, no. Please. After you. I'm happy to go, if you'd rather...

BETHANY. (*Ending her inspection.*) All right. Gorgeous. Now. We have the wine? Good. My choice of who shall stay with me ever after. My choice... My choice is...

(*Both men close their eyes. So does* **NELL**.)

G-AUNT R. Stop!

(*The* **STORYPLAYERS** *freeze.*)

UNCLE E. Why are you stopping there?

UNCLE O. It was just getting to the exciting bit.

G-AUNT R. I'm tired. It's been an exhausting story.

UNCLE E. Well, you can't stop there.

G-AUNT R. Just for a moment, I need a rest.

UNCLE O. I want to know what happens…

UNCLE E. You're impossible, Repetitus, you really are…

G-AUNT R. You finish it, then, Erraticus.

UNCLE E. Me?

G-AUNT R. If you want to. If you think you can be trusted to. There's only one more sentence. Mind you, you'll probably get that wrong, too, won't you?

UNCLE E. Of course I won't get it wrong, don't be so ridiculous…

G-AUNT R. I'm not so sure. *(Scornfully.)* Grethel and Hansel!

UNCLE E. All right, all right…

G-AUNT R. Snakes…

UNCLE O. And fingers…

G-AUNT R. And telephones…

UNCLE O. And saucepan lids…

UNCLE E. All right, all right, all right! We'll see. We shall see who can't finish a story. Here we go. Where were we?

G-AUNT R. The witch was about to choose.

UNCLE E. Yes.

G-AUNT R. Which brother she would keep for hers.

UNCLE E. Yes, yes, yes...

G-AUNT R. And we know which one she keeps, don't we, Erraticus?

UNCLE E. Yes, we do. Thank you. So to continue:

BETHANY. All right. Gorgeous. Now. We have the wine? Good. My choice of who shall stay with me ever after? My choice... My choice is—

(Both men close their eyes. So does. **NELL.***)*

(To **JENKIN.***)* —is you!

*(***BETHANY** *crosses and kisses* **JENKIN** *on the forehead. She starts to lead him away by the hand.* **JENKIN** *is in a daze.* **FRED** *opens his eyes and looks at* **NELL.***)*

G-AUNT R. *(With a scream.)* That's the wrong one. Erraticus, you fool, you've made her pick the wrong one...

UNCLE O. *(together)* You fool! You fool!

UNCLE E. All right! All right! All right! All right!

FRED. Nell!

NELL. What? What's happened?

FRED. Quickly... Come on!

NELL. Where?

FRED. Anywhere—away from here—come on...

*(***KEVIN** *produces chase music.)*

*(***FRED** *grabs* **NELL***'s hand and they start to run hither and thither to find their way out of the castle.)*

G-AUNT R. What's going on?

UNCLE E. They're running away.

UNCLE O. What are they doing?

G-AUNT R. This is all your stupid fault, Erraticus—how can you ruin a perfectly good story with one stupid sentence…

UNCLE E. It was not my fault—you just like to make things complicated. Why didn't you have a tree fall on him and have done with it…?

UNCLE O. Just a minute, I'll deal with it. Don't panic. I can deal with it! To continue. They ran up and down corridors for several minutes but they could find no way out.

FRED. There's no way out.

UNCLE O. They were lost.

NELL. We're lost.

UNCLE O. Finally, they ran through a small door and found themselves at a dead end. The door behind him slammed—

(There is a slam from **KEVIN.***)*

—shut! Jonas tried the handle—

(There is a rattle from **KEVIN.***)*

But the door had locked itself.

NELL. We're trapped!

FRED. Looks like it. I'm sorry, Nell.

NELL. Oh, Flavius!

(They cling to each other.)

UNCLE O. Stop!

*(The **PLAYERS** freeze.)*

There you are. Perfectly simple, if you know what you're doing.

G-AUNT R. Well done, Oblivious, congratulations.

UNCLE E. *(Sulkily.)* Amazing you got that far and managed to stay awake—and remembered both their names. Quite a record for you.

UNCLE O. At least I did it. Unlike some. *(To **ERRATICUS**.)* Well, do you want another try at finishing it?

UNCLE E. No, no, no, no, no. You finish it. Cleversocks.

G-AUNT R. Go on. Finish it, Oblivious. You finish it.

UNCLE O. If you insist. Thank you, Great Aunt.

G-AUNT R. You know what to do?

UNCLE O. Yes.

G-AUNT R. You fetch the witch...

UNCLE O. Yes, yes...

G-AUNT R. To kiss the boy...

UNCLE O. *(Impatiently.)* Yes, yes, yes...

UNCLE E. What about the girl?

G-AUNT R. Oh, she might as well kiss her as well. Let's get rid of both of them. They're both infernal nuisances...

UNCLE O. Do you mind? Am I telling this story, or aren't I?

G-AUNT R. Go on then.

UNCLE O. Right. *(He pauses slightly.)* Where were we?

UNCLE E. Oh, dear heavens...

G-AUNT R. We were here:

(The characters reanimate.)

NELL. We're trapped.

FRED. Looks like it. I'm sorry, Nell.

NELL. Oh, Flavius.

UNCLE O. Oh, yes. And as they stood there, they heard the sound of the witch's footsteps coming slowly along the passage towards them.

*(There are hollow footsteps from **KEVIN**.)*

They both looked around but there was no escape.

FRED. There's no escape.

UNCLE O. The footsteps stopped, the handle turned—

*(There is a door handle rattle from **KEVIN**.)*

—the door slowly opened—

*(There is a door creak from **KEVIN**.)*

—and there stood the witch.

*(**BETHANY** appears.)*

BETHANY. Did you know there was an old saying. It's a witch's privilege to change her mind. I've just changed mine. I've let your brother go, wasn't that kind of me? Instead, I now choose— *(She points a finger at **FRED**.)*

*(**FRED** closes his eyes.)*

You!

NELL. *(Softly.)* No, you can't—you mustn't—you can't—

BETHANY. Can't? Can't! What's can't? Why can't I? Who's to stop me?

NELL. Me.

BETHANY. How? How?

NELL. *(Quietly.)* Because—because I love him…

BETHANY. *(Murmuring sweetly.)* Too bad, child. Too bad.

(NELL closes her eyes.)

UNCLE O. And the witch stepped forward, took the boy by the hands and kissed…kissed him on the… oh, dammit what's the word…thingy…kissed him on the thingy…

G-AUNT R. *(Screaming with fury.)* Oblivious!

UNCLE E. *(Likewise.)* Oblivious!

G-AUNT R.		You fool! How could you go wrong with that? It was all set up for you…
UNCLE E.	*(Together.)*	I knew he'd make a mess of it. He always does…
UNCLE O.		What's the word? What's the stupid word? Just one word, that's all it was…

(During this FRED opens his eyes. BETHANY stands frozen waiting for the sentence to be completed, halfway through a kiss that has never been planted.)

FRED. Nell!

NELL. *(Opening her eyes.)* Flavius—What's—?

FRED. Come on—quickly...

NELL. I think I've remembered a way out—

FRED. Where?

NELL. Through the kitchens, follow me...

(More chase music from **KEVIN.** **FRED** *and* **NELL** *start to run as before.)*

UNCLE E. What's happening now?

UNCLE O. What are they doing?

G-AUNT R. Theyre getting away again, you idiots...

UNCLE E. Stop them!

UNCLE O. Stop them!

G-AUNT R Stop them!

NELL. Here we are, through here...

FRED. We're out! We're in the forest...

UNCLE E. They're outside!

UNCLE O. They've got into the forest!

UNCLE E. They've escaped!

UNCLE O. What are we going to do?

G-AUNT R. Don't worry, leave it to me... It always has to be me in the end, doesn't it? And even as they ran through the forest—a great wind arose...

(There is a howling wind noise from **KEVIN.**)*

And try as they might, they could not run against such a wind. They found themselves being blown backwards...back...towards the castle...

NELL. Flavius, help me…hold on…

FRED. It's no good…it's too strong… I can't…

G-AUNT R. And then the whole forest was alive with whirling leaves and twisting twigs and stinging sticks and bristling branches which tore and scratched at them as if trying to cling on to them for ever… and the hurricane grew stronger and stronger and stronger until suddenly—

(**KEVIN** *makes a loud creaking sound.*)

NELL. Look out! Mind the tree!

FRED. Watch out for the tree!

G-AUNT R. And the highest tree in the forest came crashing down on top of them both.

(*There is a final crash. The wind dies. Silence.*)

(**FRED** *and* **NELL** *lie motionless on the ground.*)

(*Satisfied.*) There!

UNCLE E. Are they—?

UNCLE O. Dead?

G-AUNT R. Oh, no… Not yet…

NELL. (*Groggily.*) Flavius—?

FRED. Uh?

NELL. Can you move? I can't move—something's… The tree's on top of me… I can't move.

FRED. Just a minute, I'll—I'll try and…

G-AUNT R. But try as they might, they could never hope to move the tree. And as they lay there, they heard someone coming towards them, singing...

BETHANY. *(Singing, offstage.)*
AS LOUD AS YOU SCREAM,
AS MUCH AS YOU SHOUT,
ONCE YOU'RE IN HERE, YOU WILL NEVER GET OUT,
WITHOUT ANY DOUBT, YOU WILL NEVER GET OUT,
NEVER GET OUT, NEVER GET OUT...

NELL. *(In a whisper.)* It's the witch...

FRED. The witch...

NELL. I love you, Flavius...

FRED. I love you, Nell...

(BETHANY appears.)

BETHANY. Hallo, kids. What's the problem here?

NELL. We're trapped, can you...? Could you...? Please?

BETHANY. Good heavens, yes. Oh dear. Hang about. Hup!

G-AUNT R. And with her little finger the witch lifted the tree off them...

*(There are more creaks from **KEVIN**.)*

BETHANY. Hey *voilà*!

FRED. *(Trying to rise.)* Thank you. We're so—

BETHANY. No, no... Please. Don't get up. You must rest, both of you. You look so sweet lying there. Do you know what you remind me of? Babes in the Wood. You lie there and sleep.

(She bends low over them.)

And if you're both specially good—you'll get a goodnight kiss. Like this...

(She kisses **NELL** *on the forehead.)*

...and this...

(She kisses **FRED**.*)*

...There!

G-AUNT R. And as the witch kissed them both on their foreheads—

UNCLE O. *(Muttering.)* Foreheads! That's the word...

G-AUNT R. *(Glaring at him.)* ...and as she kissed them she drew from inside their heads all the secret dreams they'd ever dreamt and all the secret loves they'd ever treasured. And pursing her lips, she blew them clear away into the bright morning air... Then Molly no longer remembered Jonas... and Jonas forgot Molly. And likewise Flavius forgot Nell and Nell forgot Flavius... So for each of them, the other no longer existed...

UNCLE E. Brilliant!

UNCLE O. Bravo!

G-AUNT R. *(Rising.)* And the StoryPlayers, their tale told, gathered up their belongings and departed slowly for another place, for another story...

(The **PLAYERS**, *except for* **FRED**, *slowly leave the stage.* **ALBERT** *replaces the sign that says, "Stories told here today at 10.30 a.m." They are followed by the* **STORYTELLERS**, *moving as they speak.)*

G-AUNT R. And not one of them remembered Flavius. Nor did Flavius remember them. In fact, wherever he was, the witch had taken so much of his memory, he couldn't even remember his own name. Indeed, he became convinced that his name was Fred.

UNCLE E. Fred?

UNCLE O. Fred?

G-AUNT R. Why not? It's as good a name as any other.

(They all go out, leaving **FRED** *sitting as at the start.)*

FRED. *(To no-one in particular.)* I've been waiting here a very long time indeed. *(He reflects.)* At least, I think I have.

*(***NELL** *enters. She carries her bundle as before.)*

NELL. *(Seeing* **FRED.***)* Oh, hallo.

FRED. Hallo.

NELL. Why, it's... Isn't it...? Yes. Aren't you—?

FRED. Fred.

NELL. No, you're not. Surely you're...?

FRED. Fred. My name's Fred.

NELL. Well. All right, then. I'm Nell.

FRED. How do you do?

NELL. Fred? *(She stares at him.)* Are you sure that's your name?

FRED. Don't start that again, please.

NELL. Strange. It must have been another story, mustn't it?

FRED. What?

NELL. Another time. Yes. It was a happy time, I know that.

FRED. *(Suspecting she is slightly deranged.)* Oh, yes? Good.

NELL. So anyway what story are you in at the moment, Fred?

FRED. Story? I'm not in a story.

NELL. Oh, but you must be.

FRED. What story?

NELL. Whoever's telling it. The story by the person who made you up.

FRED. Made me up? What are you talking about?

NELL. Invented you. The reason you're here is because someone somewhere is telling a story about you. You knew that, surely? If you don't mind my saying so, you're not very well informed, are you, Fred? You don't seem to know much.

FRED. I know plenty of things, never you mind.

NELL. What, for instance? You don't even look as if you know what you're doing here.

FRED. I know what I'm doing here.

NELL. What?

FRED. I'm doing here—waiting—waiting patiently for these stories to start. When are they going to start? I've been waiting here for ages.

NELL. How long? Exactly?

FRED. *(Puzzled.)* I don't know. Exactly. Does it matter? Hours and hours. Days and days. I don't know. Years and years. For ever.

NELL. For ever after. Fascinating. You know, I'm not certain yet if I'm appearing in your story or you're appearing in my story. But the fact is we're both in the same story now. Obviously. And the story is apparently that I should come on here ahead of the others in order to meet you alone. Presumably. Why?

FRED. No idea.

NELL. Why to meet you? There must have been a reason. We shall see, won't we? This must have an ending or they couldn't have started it. How exciting... Which one of them could possibly have told it like this? It must have been one of them...

FRED. One of who?

NELL Well, either...

(Before she can answer, though, the other **STORYPLAYERS, BETHANY, TALITHA, JENKIN** *and* **ALBERT** *enter as before.)*

NELL. Ah! Here they are...

BETHANY. Here we are.

JENKIN. Here we are.

TALITHA. Here we are.

ALBERT. Are we? Thank heavens.

NELL. Everyone, this is Fred.

JENKIN. *(Coolly.)* Oh, yes?

TALITHA. Oh, how lovely. Another character.

BETHANY. *(Looking* **FRED** *up and down appreciatively.)* Another character. Delicious.

ALBERT. Not before time.

FRED. Hallo...

NELL. Fred, this is Bethany...

BETHANY. Hallo. He seems familiar, doesn't he?

TALITHA. Yes, he does rather. I'm Talitha, hallo.

FRED. *(A bit overwhelmed.)* Hallo.

TALITHA. But I can't think where we could have met him, Bethany, can you?

BETHANY. No. But he's not someone you'd forget, is he Talitha?

TALITHA. Not at all.

BETHANY. *(To* **NELL.***)* What did you say his name was, Nell?

NELL. Fred.

BETHANY. Fred?

TALITHA. Fred?

BETHANY. No.

TALITHA. No.

ALBERT. I knew a Fred once.

NELL. Did you?

ALBERT. *(Indicating* **FRED.***)* But it wasn't this one.

NELL. No?

ALBERT. No, this particular Fred died when he was fifty-seven. Eaten by a giant.

TALITHA. Sad.

JENKIN. Personally, I have never known anyone called Fred, alive or dead. But you are familiar... *(He walks away and starts to unpack his bundle in a distant corner.)*

FRED. Good. Well, are we—? Are you all going to tell us a story then. Now you're here?

(They all look at him blankly.)

Please?

ALBERT. Oh, no.

BETHANY. No.

NELL. No.

TALITHA. No.

JENKIN. Certainly not.

BETHANY. We're not the StoryTellers...

NELL. We're the StoryPlayers.

BETHANY. Quite different.

TALITHA. Quite, quite different.

ALBERT. Quite, quite, quite different.

FRED. All right then, who is telling these stories, if you're not?

TALITHA. They are, of course.

BETHANY. Who else?

FRED. Who?

NELL. Either Great Aunt Repetitus...

ALBERT. If you like hearing things twice...

TALITHA. Or Uncle Erraticus...

ALBERT. When he can remember to get it right...

BETHANY. Or Uncle Oblivious...

ALBERT. If he can remember anything at all.

TALITHA. He forgot on the way here.

BETHANY. That's why we're late.

NELL. *(To* **FRED.***)* Don't worry, they'll be along shortly.

TALITHA. They're quite elderly.

BETHANY. Extremely elderly.

JENKIN. They're all half dead. Well, I'm ready. I don't know about the rest of you.

TALITHA. Well, now you're going to have to wait, Jenkin, aren't you?

NELL. Because the StoryTellers aren't here, are they?

BETHANY. Why don't you make one up yourself, Jenkin?

TALITHA. Yes, off you go, Jenkin.

NELL. Come on, Jenkin...

ALBERT. Go for it, Jenkin.

JENKIN. If you think I'm doing anything just so you lot can snigger... I can wait. Anyway, we haven't even got... Where is he?

BETHANY. *(Alarmed.)* Oh no...

ALBERT. *(Equally so.)* Oh.

NELL. *(Alarmed.)* Oh no...

JENKIN. *(Equally so.)* Oh!

FRED. What's the matter?

TALITHA. *(Agitatedly.)* Oh, oh, oh...

NELL. *(To* **JENKIN.***)* What have you done with him?

FRED. Done with who?

NELL. Kevin on Keyboards, of course.

ALBERT. What are we going to do?

NELL. Now, don't panic. Everyone spread out and look for him.

ALBERT. Spread out!

TALITHA. Spread out!

BETHANY. Spread out!

JENKIN. Spread out!

(They all spread out.)

FRED. *(Still mystified.)* I'm still not quite certain who we're looking for.

NELL. Kevin on Keyboards. Who do you think? Honestly! Don't you know anything?

ALBERT. Kevin on Keyboards! Come on, call him, you lot.

BETHANY. Kevin on Keyboards!

NELL. Kevin on Keyboards!

TALITHA. Kevin on Keyboards!

JENKIN. Kevin on Keyboards!

FRED. Kevin on Keyboards! *(To* **NELL.***)* What does he look like?

NELL. Well, obviously he looks exactly like...

BETHANY. Shhh!

TALITHA. Listen!

ALBERT. Shhh!

JENKIN. Shh! Everyone.

(We hear a distant squeaking noise, approaching.)

NELL. That's him. *(Calling.)* Kevin on Keyboards!

ALL. *(Shouting.)* Kevin on Keyboards!

(There is the roar of an engine, the squeal of tyres and **KEVIN ON KEYBOARDS** *arrives. He screeches to a halt at the end of the stage.)*

FRED. *(Recovering from the sight.)* What is it?

NELL. Kevin on Keyboards.

ALBERT. This is Kevin. This is his keyboard.

FRED. Is he a StoryTeller?

BETHANY. Not really, no.

TALITHA. But he does help tell the stories, don't you, Kevin?

*(***KEVIN** *presses a note and a voice from somewhere says "You bet I do, honeychile.")*

NELL. Kevin, this is Fred.

FRED. Hallo, Kevin, how do you do.

*(***KEVIN** *presses a key and plays a chorus of "Hallo"s.)*

BETHANY. That's just his way of saying hallo.

TALITHA. I think he likes you.

FRED. *(To* **KEVIN.***)* You know, he seems familiar. I've met him before.

NELL. Have you? That's interesting. Where?

FRED. I can't think where.

NELL. Try and think, Fred. It could be important.

ALBERT. *(To* **FRED.***)* Were you ever a woodcutter? Maybe that's where we've met?

FRED. No. I don't think so.

ALBERT. A miller? A blacksmith? A magic shoemaker?

FRED. No. I'm sure I'd have remembered.

NELL. He doesn't remember anything, Albert. Who is he? Why do we all know him?

TALITHA. Someone should have given him some thoughts, surely?

BETHANY. And memories...

TALITHA. And ideas.

BETHANY. Careless. It wouldn't have taken long, would it?

ALBERT. As the Swineherd once said to me... Ideas cost nothing.

NELL. *(Touching* **FRED** *lightly on the cheek.)* You poor thing. We'll find out about you. Don't worry.

FRED. *(Frowning, taking her hand.)* Nell...?

NELL. Yes? What is it, Fred?

FRED. Nell... Oh, Nell... *(He looks round the group.)* Bethany...?

BETHANY. Yes...

FRED. Talitha?

TALITHA. Yes.

BETHANY. He's remembering...

NELL. Sssh!

FRED. Albert...?

ALBERT. That's me.

FRED. Jenkin...?

JENKIN. Yes.

NELL. Who are you? Who are you really, Fred...?

FRED. I'm F—Fl—Flav—ius. Fla—vius...

NELL. Flavius?

BETHANY. Flavius?

TALITHA. Flavius?

ALBERT. Flavius?

JENKIN. Flavius?

NELL. *(Overjoyed.)* Oh, Flavius...

(**NELL** *throws her arms round* **FRED**. **FRED** *is a little bewildered.*)

ALBERT. *(With a whoop.)* Flavius!

BETHANY. *(Likewise.)* Flavius!

TALITHA. *(Likewise.)* Flavius!

JENKIN. *(Likewise.)* Flavius!

(**KEVIN** *strikes up a wild jig.* **ALBERT**, **BETHANY**, **TALITHA** *and* **JENKIN** *dance wildly for a moment.* **NELL** *and* **FRED** *watch, amused.*)

FRED. Just a minute! Just a minute! Before we celebrate too soon. Remember, we are not, as they say, clear of the wood. We have not yet dealt with the StoryTellers. They are still telling stories for us and they are capable of telling more.

ALBERT. True.

TALITHA. What do we do?

NELL. Flavius?

JENKIN. Flavius?

FRED. Leave them to me...

(**KEVIN** *plays a fanfare.*)

ALBERT. Here they come!

BETHANY. Here they come!

TALITHA. Here they come!

JENKIN. Here they come!

NELL. They're coming.

(*They all stand back respectfully.* **FRED** *follows suit.*)

(*The* **STORYTELLERS** *enter together as before.*)

(*The* **PLAYERS** *stand motionless, waiting.*)

G-AUNT R. Here we are, then.

UNCLE E. Here we are.

UNCLE O. Here we are.

G-AUNT R. Time for stories!

UNCLE E. Stories!

UNCLE O. Stories!

(**KEVIN** *plays a fanfare. During the following, the three* **STORYTELLERS** *hobble to their positions outside the acting area where they seat themselves. The* **PLAYERS** *gather at the edge of the stage, and wait expectantly.* **FRED** *stands with them.*)

ALBERT. *(Cheerfully.)* What happens now?

NELL. What do we do next?

BETHANY. What's going to happen?

TALITHA. Flavius?

JENKIN. Flavius?

FRED. Shhh!

G-AUNT R. And the first story will be told by... *(She pauses dramatically.)*

NELL. Wait for it!

FRED. Me.

G-AUNT R. What?

UNCLE E. What?

UNCLE O. What?

G-AUNT R. How dare you!

UNCLE O. Who is he?

UNCLE E. No idea.

FRED. Once upon a time, there were three old Story Tellers—Great Aunt Repetitus, Uncle Erraticus and Uncle Oblivious—

G-AUNT R. Eh?

UNCLE E. Eh?

UNCLE O. Eh?

FRED. —and these three StoryTellers had so outlived their welcome that they decided never to tell stories again. Ever.

UNCLE O. What's he saying? What's he saying?

FRED. And so Uncle Oblivious said to the Players:

UNCLE O. I'm awfully sorry. I'm not going to tell any more stories ever—I'm just going to go and lie down for the next one hundred and fifty years if you'll excuse me... What am I saying? I'm not saying that. Who's saying this... Goodbye... Who am I saying? I'm not saying this. Goodbye. Not goodbye. Yes, goodbye.

PLAYERS. Goodbye!

(**UNCLE OBLIVIOUS** *goes off, looking rather dazed.*)

FRED. And then Uncle Erraticus, who had been watching all this—

UNCLE E. Oh, no, oh, no. Not with me you don't, young man...

FRED. —decided it was time to stretch his legs and up he got and almost immediately he banged his foot.

UNCLE E. (*Doing so.*) Ow!

FRED. And then, would you believe, his knee.

UNCLE E. Ooo!

G-AUNT R. Erraticus!

FRED. And then his head.

UNCLE E. Ouch!

FRED. And then his elbow!

UNCLE E. Oook!

G-AUNT R. Erraticus! What are you playing at?

FRED. Which made him hop up and down like a deranged rabbit.

UNCLE E. *(Hopping about.)* You can't do this to me—I forbid it!

FRED. And, would you believe it, the poor man jumped up and down so furiously that eventually his trousers caught fire.

(Smoke starts to come from **UNCLE ERRATICUS**.*)*

G-AUNT R. Erraticus!

UNCLE E. Oh, no, no, no... Help...

FRED. And he ran from that building and into the nearby duck pond and was never seen again. Bye!

*(***UNCLE ERRATICUS** *dashes off.)*

PLAYERS. Goodbye!

*(***FRED** *turns to* **GREAT-AUNT REPETITUS**.*)*

G-AUNT R. I hope you don't think you can frighten me, young man, because you can't. I'm a far better story teller than you are. If you don't believe it, try me...

FRED. You're not that good.

G-AUNT R. Good enough for you.

FRED. Why do you think I'm still here? Why hasn't Flavius disappeared like you planned for him to disappear? Ever after? Tell me that?

G-AUNT R. You're still here because one of those two old fools made a mistake… Probably Oblivious. He forgot. He's always forgetting. He forgets everything. He brought you back.

FRED. It wasn't Uncle Oblivious.

G-AUNT R. Erraticus then. What does it matter? Erraticus made one of his mistakes. He makes mistakes all the time. You're another of them…

FRED. He's not the one, either.

G-AUNT R. Who else? Who else could possibly…? *(She stares at him.)* Me? Don't be ridiculous.

FRED. Remember, you're the one who tells stories that go in circles. You're the one who kept bringing me back—and back—and back…

G-AUNT R. It can't be… It can't be me…

FRED. It is…

G-AUNT R. I don't—I don't believe you…

FRED. And so Great Aunt Repetitus started to tell her last story…

G-AUNT R. You're lying…you're a little liar…

FRED. There was once…

G-AUNT R. There was once…you can't do this to me…

FRED. An old woman…

G-AUNT R. An old woman…

FRED. Who told stories that went round and round…

G-AUNT R. Round and round…

FRED. And that was all there was…

G-AUNT R. And that was all there was an old woman who told stories that went round and round and that was all there was once an old woman who told stories that went round and round and that was all there was once…*etc.*

(She goes off, still reciting her tale and getting faster and faster. **KEVIN** *accelerates her story even more.)*

FRED. Bye!

PLAYERS. *(To the retreating* **GREAT-AUNT REPETITUS.***)* Goodbye!

ALBERT. Free!

BETHANY. Free!

TALITHA. Free!

JENKIN. Free!

NELL. We're free.

FRED. Wait! One last story. A very short one… Are you all ready?

ALL. Ready.

FRED. Once upon a time…

ALL. Once upon a time…

FRED. There was a group of players…

ALL. There was a group of players…

FRED. Albert…

ALBERT. Albert…

FRED. Bethany....

BETHANY. Bethany...

FRED. Talitha....

TALITHA. Talitha...

FRED. Jenkin...

JENKIN. Jenkin...

FRED. Kevin on Keyboards...

(**KEVIN** *plays: **"KEVIN ON KEYBOARDS"**.*)

And not forgetting Nell...

NELL. Not forgetting Nell...

FRED. And they all, every one of them lived—

ALL. —every one of them lived—

FRED. —happily—

ALL. —happily—

FRED. —ever—

ALL. —ever—AFTER!

(And with a whoop they all run off.)

(Curtain.)

ABOUT THE AUTHOR

Alan Ayckbourn has worked in theatre as a playwright and director for over fifty years, rarely if ever tempted by television or film, which perhaps explains why he continues to be so prolific. To date he has written more than 79 plays, many one act plays and a large amount of work for the younger audience. His work has been translated into over 35 languages, is performed on stage and television throughout the world and has won countless awards.

Major successes include: *Relatively Speaking, How the Other Half Loves, Absurd Person Singular, Bedroom Farce, A Chorus of Disapproval*, and *The Norman Conquests*. In recent years, there have been revivals of *Season's Greetings* and *A Small Family Business* at the National theatre, in the West End *Absent Friends, A Chorus of Disapproval, Relatively Speaking* and *How the Other Half Loves*. In 2015, Chichester mounted a very successful revival of Way Upstream.

Artistic Director of the Stephen Joseph theatre from 1972 – 2009 where almost all his plays have been first staged, he continues to direct his latest new work there. In recent years, he has been inducted into American Theatre's Hall of Fame, received the 2010 Critics' Circle Award for Services to the Arts and became the first British playwright to receive both Olivier and Tony Special Lifetime Achievement Awards. He was knighted in 1997 for services to the theatre.

www.ingramcontent.com/pod-product-compliance
Ingram Content Group UK Ltd.
Pitfield, Milton Keynes, MK11 3LW, UK
UKHW021839210426
5322IPUK00022B/372